# Postcoloniality, Globalization, and Diaspora

# Postcoloniality, Globalization, and Diaspora

## *What's Next?*

### Edited by Ashmita Khasnabish

LEXINGTON BOOKS
Lanham • Boulder • New York • London

Published by Lexington Books
An imprint of The Rowman & Littlefield Publishing Group, Inc.
4501 Forbes Boulevard, Suite 200, Lanham, Maryland 20706
www.rowman.com

6 Tinworth Street, London SE11 5AL

British Library Cataloguing in Publication Information Available

**Library of Congress Cataloging-in-Publication Data Available**

ISBN 978-1-4985-7023-7 (cloth)
ISBN 978-1-4985-7025-1(pbk)
ISBN 978-1-4985-7024-4 (electronic)

To my dearest Parents and to Bhumip, Inrava, and Srijesa.

# Contents

# Acknowledgments

It was quite a challenging and pleasant journey from 2013 up until now, to complete *Postcoloniality, Globalization, and Diaspora: What's Next?* The seed of this project was sown in 2013 at the Northeastern Modern Language Association Conference in Boston with the panel "Rethinking the Concept of the Postcolonial," which initially inspired it, since as Humanities scholars we were brainstorming vigorously about the next step of the postcolonial. It matured more in the following year in the NeMLA panel "Postcoloniality, Globalization, and Diaspora: What's Next?" which offered me the title of the book. Then it grew over the years and as part of this journey, I would like to mention my trip to Oxford University as a visiting scholar last summer, as its ambience gave me the idea of writing my chapter on Rabindranath Tagore's play *Red Oleanders* with its theme of the dissolution of the master-slave dialectic, which got further accentuated by going to Grundy, Virginia, and seeing the coal mines. The inspiration derived from the NeMLA panels as well as the travelling made this book happen. In this artistic and political venture joined not only my panelists but my international colleagues from Ireland to Mauritius (now in Cape Town) and from the United States.

I pay my special homage first to Dr. Ifyeani Menkiti who passed away in June 2019 but was very warmly behind the project until his death. I remember my last conversation with him as I was leaving for India and he insisted that I take down the note over phone. I am glad I did; that was our last conversation. He added more thoughts to one of his comments on John Rawls's notion of the "second or the global original position" and its relation to his notion of the "ethical commonwealth."

My warmest thanks go to all the contributors of this anthology for their hard work and the sense of belonging together. Writing emails to Melanie (Dr. Melanie Otto) and Markus (Dr. Markus Arnold) and getting instantaneous responses with whatever question I had for them was marvelous for increasing the bond. Stephanie (Dr. Sephanie Matthews Walsh) came to NeMLA not just to give her paper in my panel on Nomadology but to honor our forthcoming anthology. Paget (Dr. Paget Henry) honored the volume with a book-length chapter. Aida's chapter drew me to it for its specific focus on the theme of the book.

I offer my heartfelt thanks to all the editors of Lexington Books for their support throughout this long process. I also offer warm thanks to my two daughters and my husband for their encouragement and support; especially I offer a special thanks to my younger daughter Srijesa Khasnabish for her constant encouragement for the project and sometimes criticism which was conducive to the process of completion. I offer thanks to my dear father who is looking at the anthology from his heavenly home, to my mother who sent me abroad to fulfill my First Girl's dream, and to my sister Aurobi.

Finally, I offer my precious thanks to Dr. Rebecca Kennedy, the former Chair of the Humanities Department at Lasell College (now University), for her inspirational support to encourage me while I received the book contract and also for the completion of the project.

# Introduction

*Postcoloniality, Diaspora, and Globalization:
What's Next?*

## Ashmita Khasnabish

The anthology *Postcoloniality, Globalization, and Diaspora: What's Next?* proposes a futuristic vision about what we are moving from—what we call our postcolonial existence and its aftermath, diaspora—and the continuation, which we define as *globalization*. This volume is a very special and significant collection of chapters devoted to that inquiry, some of which arose from the panels I organized though the Northeastern Modern Language Association over the past few years. I would like to mention two panels: "Rethinking the Concept of the Postcolonial," held in Boston in 2013, and "Postcoloniality, Diaspora, and Globalization: What's Next?" These panels contribute significantly to this volume, apart from my American and European colleagues and contributors.

The inspiration for this volume is my panel and my paper entitled "Philosophical Afterthoughts." It was quite astonishing to listen to Obama's Nobel Prize lecture a few years ago, when he mentioned the situation in which one has to go to war in order to defend oneself. Three aspects of the speech were stunning. Obama mentioned the term *soft power*, he mentioned the need for the League of Nations in the past, and he mentioned that when everything fails, one has to go to war in self-defense. His statement immediately brought to my mind two names: Joseph Nye and Sri Aurobindo. Joseph Nye came to mind because of his book *Soft Power*; it seems that Obama derived his philosophical concepts from Nye's book. Sri Aurobindo, the Indian freedom fighter and Cambridge-educated litterateur-cum-philosopher living in exile and writing books, speaks in *The Ideal of Human Unity* about the notion of the League of Nations and the significance of nurturing the notion of world peace.

In the chapter "Philosophical Politics" of my recent monograph *Negotiating Capability and Diaspora: A Philosophical Politics*, I suggest that we need a psychological unity to achieve world peace or move toward it. I offer the theories of two philosophers: John Rawls and Amartya Sen. What is unique about Rawls's theory is that he tries to synthesize the *comprehensive doctrines* and the notion of political justice. What are these comprehensive doctrines? Comprehensive doctrines refer to human beings' emotional, ethnic, and religious affiliations. He proposes that we abandon our sense of other people's differences and compromise, achieving unity for the sake of political justice. Sen's reservation is that if we eradicate differences, there could be pernicious effects: eradicating other people's identities. It is quite a paradox; Sen counters Rawls's theory with his own theory of *capability*. He refers to the Buddhist *Sutta Nipata* and highlights the message that if we can do good for the world, we must; according to the capability approach, our action will be determined by our value system. The key words are *reason to value*.

Postcoloniality should be the ideal state of bliss and freedom: Homi Bhava offers us the discourse of hybridity, and Spivak offers us her book *The Critique of Postcolonial Reason*. But the lacuna is that no one has offered us any trajectory, beyond simply describing it, that will take us beyond the notions of hybridity and postcolonial reason. *Hybridity* has been replaced by the term *transnational*, but still the ontology is missing. In my LexMedia television interview, Noam Chomsky talks about this, asking me if I want an optimistic or a realistic answer. What is wrong with optimism? In this regard, I find Fanon highly optimistic. . . . He alludes to consciousness in almost every chapter of the book *Black Skin, White Masks*. He also refers to the terms *transcendence* and *ontology*; he talks about overcoming the problem. I would say that we have reached a time at which, if we do not mention optimism, the world will move to extinction. We go back to our countries. We travel without a passport. We practice ethics.

My volume addresses an ontological problem: the problem is that of master-slave dialectic or the oppression of one group by another group in a way that is dominated by master-slave hierarchy or dialectic. Postcoloniality, diaspora, and globalization: all of these phenomena have already occurred; they are already constructed. We now need to envision *what's next?* We have postmodernism, postcolonialism, neo-colonialism, neo-liberalism—all these are terms, and all the contributors have delved into these terms in depth. But what I propose is a vision of the world where the power struggle will be reduced or removed, as can occur, perhaps, through the liberation and dissolution of bad ego and the transformation of consciousness. Sri Aurobindo's philosophy of the *religion of humanity* is very alluring as a solution to this humanitarian issue. I am seeking a solution for the problem that occurs through discrimination, where one party looks down upon the other. If one looks through history, one can find many such moments of discrimination that are beyond the reach of my knowledge or that of any single human being; I am presenting here one poem, translating it myself to offer an example of one of these moments. The Bengali poet Jagadish Chandra Das writes these lines (I am translating):

> Why cannot I unite the earth and the sky?
> The more the sky becomes wide
> The earth shrinks and your relatives get lost.
> In the coal mine.
> Just like the laborers of the coal mine of Ratibari [a specific place the poet is referencing]
> Being underground-locked for one hundred twenty-five hours in darkness
> . . .
> My sisters, villagers, relatives, neighbors of my country
> They are also imprisoned within the cave of Pakistan
> They did not die, but sucked in the life of death before death
> One day death will come, but did not yet, their hope did not die, did not get extinguished.

This poem, with its intense tone, reminds me of Sashi Tharoor's speech on "Britain Owes Reparations to India." The poem is set up in the context of the Partition of India: in the poem, we can feel excruciating pain through the coal mine imagery. Partition caused the separation between the poet and his family, and he mourns his loss. The poet is looking at this situation in the year 1969, three years prior to the 1972 independence of East Pakistan from Pakistan. But the Partition caused separation, which caused the poet so much grief, and Sashi Tharoor, in his glorious speech, points this out very clearly and energetically. What shocked me most was the economic deprivation triggered by British colonization: one of the prominent effects was the famine that killed 40 million people, and the other was Britain's 200-million-pound debt to India from World War II, which, among other atrocities, made Indian weavers poor. The poet's grief that the earth and the sky can never touch each other is very significant, as are the lines "My sisters, villagers, relatives, neighbors of my country/They are also imprisoned within the cave of Pakistan/They did not die, but sucked in the life of death before death."

Sashi Tharoor outlines the atrocities inflicted on Indians and states that the British have a moral debt to the Indians. The British offered reparations to the Maoris of New Zealand; why did they not repay the Indians of India? Tharoor, in his Oxford lecture "Britain Does Owe Reparations," gives us this sharp line with its pungent tone: "to oppress, maim, enslave, kill people for two hundred years and then say you are democratic." In Tharoor's voice and also in the poet's voice, we hear a tone of despair as well as hope. It is not simply protest we hear, but protest compounded with a note of future vision: the poet says, "One day death will come, but did not yet, their hope did not die, did not get extinguished." Tharoor very strongly and logically claims at the end of his speech that for the next two hundred years, one pound each day must be given to Indians by the British to pay off a moral debt. In this, I see a hint of a solution and a future trajectory, as the poet reveals at the end of his poem that "their hope did not die, did not get extinguished." It is almost a prophetic comment, because in 1971, three years later, East Pakistan became liberated from Pakistan.

The first chapter in this volume, "The Battle of Energy between Matter and Spirit: Does It Direct Us to a Better Universe?" strives to resolve that crisis of humanity. We can access this philosophical discourse through the symbolic play *Red Oleanders*, or *Raktakarabi* in Bengali. In Nandini's cry of agony, we hear the intense pain of the poet articulated: "King, they all say you know magic. Make him wake up for my sake." But the king does not know how to awaken, and he confesses that he knows how to put everything to death. The king here resembles the King of Death Yama of Hindu mythology and of the Indian philosopher Sri Aurobindo, in his hyper-epic *Savitri*, where Yama argues with Savitri that her husband cannot be brought back to life. I reference the chapter "Savitri and the Political Sublime" of *Humanitarian Identity and the Political Sublime: Intervention of a Postcolonial Feminist*. In Book 10, "Double Twilight," Canto 3, "The Debate of Love and Death," the god of Death poses challenges and discouragements to Savitri, asking her to return to earth without Satyvan: "Return, O child, to thy forsaken earth." Death carries on its battle with Savitri, portraying the world as a place of imperfection and falsehood: "But here are only facts and steel-bound Law. This truth I know that Satyavan is dead. . . . No magic truth can bring the dead to life" (125). This debate represents in a nutshell what the Indian philosopher Sri Aurobindo develops as the metaphysical battle between matter and spirit, or between reason and spirit, as I observe: "The debate between Yama the god of Death and Savitri is crucial to understand the battle between matter/reason and spirit in Sri Aurobindo's phenomenology" (125). So where does Savitri intersect with the cry of Nandini? Savitri defeats Yama and brings Satyvan back to life, but Nandini joins Ranjan in death, and here, death is identical with freedom from oppression, or it could be interpreted as the sacrifice of the artist from oppression or bourgeoisie.

Whereas Sri Aurobindo leans more toward metaphysics and the descent of spirituality, Tagore dwells in the realm of art and expresses the end of oppression through the proper role of an artist. However, in the ancient Indian *Upanishads*, poets are defined as seers and visionaries, possessing mystical and transcendental power. Tagore's *Red Oleanders* also reminds us, at the end, of Camus's observation regarding the role of an artist; that the artist is often a public enemy: "Every great work makes the human face more admirable and richer and this is its whole secret. . . . Yes, when modern tyranny shows us that, even when confined to his calling, the artist is a public enemy, it is right. But in this way tyranny pays its respects, through the artist, to an image of man that nothing has ever been able to crush" (59). We see that triumphant moment in *Red Oleanders* when the tyrant king himself surrenders to death in order to achieve eternal freedom.

There is a subtle distinction between Sri Aurobindo's approach and Rabindranath Tagore's approach: Tagore's approach is more literary, although it is metaphysical as well. Nandini, Ranjan, and Bishnu all follow the trajectory of freedom that can be achieved only when the voice of oppression wears off and is dismantled. This takes place, in the play, when the king—the voice of matter, death, oppressor, capitalism, whatever you want to call it—dismantles his own false kingdom. But what is tragic is that Ranjan—the voice of truth—has to be sacrificed for that liberation, and Nandini also joins him in death. Strangely, the king—the oppressor—is transformed through death as well. One can see here the Derridean metaphysics at play again: In order to achieve freedom from oppression, the king is deconstructed by our poet, where future vision is nuanced. But that vision is also reaching us through various songs performed throughout the play. In those songs, one can hear the call for a spiritual life that ends oppression. If the voice of the oppressor king is imagined here as that of British Raj, the transformation of that king, of course destroying both Ranjan and Nandini, could be conceived as a critique of British colonialism and a statement that it should be destroyed and the country should be given back to the Indians. Sri Aurobindo's hyper-epic *Savitri* should be read or could be read, as in my chapter "Savitri and the Political Sublime" of *Humanitarian Identity and the Political Sublime*, as a postcolonial text, in spite of its deeply spiritual or metaphysical inclinations. The voice of Yama could be conceived as the voice of the colonial British ruler of India back then, and Savitri as arguing with Yama to free the country. Her husband's death could be imagined as the deathly predicament of India as a colony. Savitri brings back her husband from the clutch of Death, and the nuance here is the freedom of the country at one level and, at another level, the resurrection of Satyavan—Savitri's husband. The chapter tries to resolve the battle between matter and spirit and strives to uphold the spiritual vision of the transformation of society, in which vision spirituality is part of pragmatic vision and could be implemented in day-to-day life, as I explained through my theory of the political sublime.

Thus, I feel that the spiritual and metaphysical implication of the notion of transcendence, or what I call sublimation, is an imperative for our future vision, and vindication of my belief appears in the feminist spiritual vision of the Oxford feminist philosopher Pamela Sue Anderson, in her work on Kantian space, among her other works. As intellectuals, we chatter about a better

world, but there is not much camaraderie, because there is no spiritual thinking or metaphysical soul-searching behind that chatter; Anderson mentions,
in her many articles on Kantian space and the sublime and sublimation, that
in the West, spiritual practice is not valued, and there is no communication
between feminist philosophers and feminist philosophers of religion, resonating with my view that spirituality gets lumped in with theology, which has a
negative connotation. But according to Indian philosophy, every single ob-
ject is a manifestation of Brahman or the concept of the Absolute. Thus, this
anthology aims towards finding a sublime dimension or a better harmony
among individuals and nations, and the contributors to this volume strive to
contribute in one way or another to that vision of harmony, either within the
corpus of literary theory or through philosophical analysis.

Paget Henry's chapter, "After Neo-Liberalism and Post-Structuralism:
Postcolonial Studies, Diaspora, and Globalization," offers this anthology the
greatest validation for Eastern/Indian metaphysics and philosophical theory
of what, in Indian philosophy, we call *sabda* in Brahman. In this chapter, by
deconstructing the movements called neo-colonialism, neo-liberalism, and
poststructuralism, Henry argues for a metaphysical theory of language based
on Sri Aurobindo's interpretation of the Indian philosophical theory behind
language. Consider Sri Aurobindo's observation in *The Future Poetry*:

> The Mantra too is not in its substance or its form a poetic enunciation of
> philosophic verities, but a rhythmic revelation or intuition arising out of the
> soul's sight of God and Nature and itself and of the world and of the inner
> truth—occult to the outward eye—of all that peoples it, the secrets of their life
> and being. (36)

Henry is vocal in articulating his challenge against the so-called postcolonial
theory that devalorizes the indigenous spiritual aspect of culture; he expresses this through his critique of the Spivakian framework that reduces Sri
Aurobindo's spiritual philosophy to the materialistic philosophy of the West
or Western reason. He comments, "As such Aurobindo's reading of the
Bhagavad Gita becomes a 'a de-racialized version of' the entire Hegelian
graph of spirit's journey (1993:63). This is truly a most troubling statement."
He has deep reservations against the kind of reductionist statement that Spivak is making, and he articulates his view strongly: "Particularly in the
context of a postcolonial exchange such as this, we should not just assume
that Derrida's center of arche-writing can imperially displace and replace
Aurobindo's mantric sounds. A much more egalitarian exchange between
these founding centers of language is called for here. . . . . How useful would
it be to consider Derridean deconstruction as a yoga for suspending or breaking through the maze of language?" The implication of Henry's chapter is
that reaching Brahman or the concept of the Absolute or the phase of ego-

transcendence is the supreme goal of human life, and the sound that we as human beings make is an expression of the Absolute Brahman. Indian philosophy attributes to sound a metaphysical origin similar to that in Derrida's interpretation of writing. Thus, the Derridean theory of writing and Aurobindo's interpretation of poetry should be given the same status, and Sri Aurobindo should not be reduced to a Third World scholar. But Oriental scholars sometimes diminish their work to cater to Western hegemony, and that perpetuates the master-slave dialectic and colonialism. Henry's brilliant piece gives voice to the mission statement of this volume to map a future direction.

In Markus Arnold's chapter, he plays with the terms *postcolonial* and *post-colonial*, and he strives to map a quasi-philosophical approach to the study of literature. The distinction that Arnold makes between the postcolonial and the postcolonial is remarkable. The term *post-colonial*, with the hyphen, is a rigid term, whereas *postcolonial* is a fluid term embodying the postmodernist voyeuristic aspects of the postcolonial condition. Arnold comments, "Indeed, postcolonial perspectives maybe more than others, are necessarily located at crossroads of different theoretical approaches." He further describes this as a "rhizomatic interplay of pursuits," resonating with Bill Ashcroft. It is interesting that he focuses on the term *rhizome*, because it points toward the nonlinear structure and plurality that he finds to be the characteristic features of Mauritian novels. Mauritian novels are automatically post-colonial; more significantly, they are postcolonial, as Arnold claims and explains. In order to distinguish these two terms more clearly, he engages Roland Barthes's distinction between the terms *ecrivant* (or scripter) and the *ecrivain*, or the writer. The ecrivant or scripter focuses on what is already there, whereas the ecrivain or the writer searches for new meanings and elaborations. He also grounds Mauritian literature in the triple understanding of the postcolonial. Thus it involves a negotiation within three paradigms; here, he draws on Graham Huggan's theory, which tries to construct a more pluralistic or cosmopolitan vision of the world. More than this interpretation, I find Arnold's reference to Bauman and his categorization of the literary terms *modernity* and *postmodernity* highly effective and connected to Barthes's *ecrivant* and *ecrivain* distinction. Postmodern identity has more openings and is not stagnant, as is modern identity. In the same vein, Arnold argues that postcolonial is a better category, as it subsumes everything under its canopy and suggests a journey forward in terms of becoming. Repeatedly, I hear that fascination in Arnold's chapter for the term *postcolonial* over *post-colonial*; whereas the former is emancipatory, the latter is claustrophobic. Arnold brings together Kwame Anthony, Appiah, Edward Said, and Homi Bhabha to develop this new discursive space for Mauritian novels. Homi Bhabha's distinction between the two literary terms *the pedagogical* and *the performative* runs parallel to his methodological distinction between the post-colonial and the postcolonial. Arnold discusses a number of Mauritian novelists but draws attention to the author of Indian origin Ananda Devi; he states, "Her transgressive protagonist violently defies the claims of monolithic ancestry and points towards an intercultural opening-up. With these indenture novels and their opposing views on origins, filiation, sacredness, convention and the individual, the contrast between what is called post-colonial and postcolonial can clearly be seen."

Melanie Otto's chapter, "'I'm a believer in the dance of change': Metamorphosis and Mutation in Keri Hulme's Short Fiction," resonates with Arnold's piece on the post-colonial and the postcolonial. Otto offers us a great introduction to the fiction writer Keri Hulme from New Zealand, with associations to the notion of the postcolonial, as well. Otto considers two of Keri Hulme's short stories from two different books: First, she engages in a very interesting discussion of Hulme's story "Hooks and Feelers," from *Te Kaihau/The Windeater*; she then examines "Hatchings," from *Stonefish*. "Hooks and Feelers" explores thoroughly what Otto calls "biculturalism," through the interaction between the indigenous Maori and the white settlers, called Pakeha. The story is about a family where the mother is from a Maori tribe, the father is Pakeha, and the adopted son is of mixed origin. Otto comments, "In contrast to a national narrative that seems primarily concerned with how the past affects the present and how cultural identities are formed with reference to an often fixed historical discourse, Hulme's fiction presents us with a vision of a protean world, abundant with a 'perverse generativity,' a term I borrow from Marina Warner" (Warner 2002, 76). Faithful to this quotation from Warner, Otto depicts mixed cultural identity, which is constructed through Hulme's characters in "Hooks and Feelers" from an innovative perspective, where a postcolonial reading intersects with the philosophical nuance of Emmanuel Levinas, in which the religious implications are transcended. An additional stance is that of environmentalism. Otto suggests that Hulme critiques the divisive legacies of biculturalism; through its inner connection with insect metamorphosis, the story symbolically represents the "creation and embrace of differences," resonating with the theme of the anthology. Hulme's passion for environmentalism and the correlation between men and insects is further explored by Otto in her discussion of "Hatchings," from the collection *Stonefish*. And through the connection of moth imagery, the story indicates a way out of cultural division and cacophony. In terms of future vision, readers will acquaint themselves through this chapter with the important relationship between postcoloniality and environmentalism and the trend in postcolonial literature in New Zealand.

Stephanie Matthew Walsh's chapter "Magical Realism: Narrative Play and Historical Jokes" is unique because it is enriched with the philosophical analysis of the concept of magical realism, drawing inner connections between this literary term and postcolonialism; it addresses the important question of the anthology and maps a trajectory and an almost nouveau interpretation of the term *magical realism*. The Canadian scholar Linda Hutcheon has interpreted magical realism in terms of postmodernism, but Walsh's interpretation is complex and striking. Her intense philosophical analysis compares Gabriel Garcia Marquez's novel *One Hundred Years of Solitude* and the Quebecois novelist Francois Barcelo's *The Tribe*. Walsh writes,

> The invitation to compare these two texts comes from Francois Barcelo's dedication to Marquez at the start of his novel. In fact, *The Tribe* serves as a Quebecois palimpsest to Marquez's *One Hundred Years of Solitude*. . . . Four striking features are worth noting. The first is the level of amplification; the second, the playful use of real historical and temporal markers; the third, the role of the writer and finally, doubles and multiples of characters. (7)

What Walsh emphasizes most is the importance of the historical and political implications of magical realism, because the subversion takes place through these methods, depoliticizing and dehistoricizing the hierarchy of colonialism. Time is also magnified to supernatural proportions: Marquez's epic tells "the story over one hundred years in the fictitious off-the-path village of Macondo." And Barcelo's *The Tribe* extends beyond 25,000 years. *The Tribe* tells the story of Canada's first tribes, led by the chief Big Nose, who is unfortunately beyond death. Barcelo's time span is thousands of years, from the Ice Age to Quebec's referendum. Walsh quotes the Quebecois critic Marie Vautier and suggests, "Barcelo is playing with the temporal organization of history to destabilize the recognizable mimetic elements" (8).

The next chapter in the volume, "Revising the Myth: A Proposal for a Methodological Protocol for the Study of American Culture," by Aida Roldan Garcia, is unique in advancing this intellectual argumentation, or what we call in Bengali *tarka*; the study arose as part of the main panel "Postcoloniality, Globalization, and Diaspora: What's Next?" and is important in advancing the theoretical debate on a future vision. Garcia observes, "Because of my previous experience in the study of culture and identity formation, I know that the study of a culture is a complex process" (1). I admire this comment, as she emphasizes the complexity of culture. In her protocol for the study of American culture, she introduces the notion of interdisciplinarity and the term *methodological plurality*, which "will give scholars access to meanings" from a pluralistic point of view; she draws here on the work of Henry Nash Smith. She proposes and advocates strongly for an investigation that goes beyond quantitative and objective approaches; her exploration therefore has ontological underpinnings. Garcia comes up with her own categories: "interdisciplinarity, the transnational turn, the domestic focus and border." It seems that the interdisciplinary approach advances dialogue, discussion, and research on qualitative approaches, and she highlights its importance. Garcia also valorizes feminist cultural studies as a concrete example in which the synthesis of qualitative and quantitative analyses can enrich the study of American culture or artifacts. She also points out the twofold outcome of feminist cultural studies: the critique of patriarchy and the presentation of positive models.

Garcia explains that the transnational category emphasizes power structure; she shows how the neoliberal capitalist apparatus controls wealth distribution, how transitional organizations organize society, and how discourses on race, gender, class, and ethnicities are formulated. The transnational approach is clearly pertinent to interdisciplinarity and to cultural discourse. In her discourse on domesticity, she follows Donald E. Pease and suggests that social, political, and cultural processes be studied at a domestic level as well. Developing her point on domesticity, she emphasizes the importance of ethnic studies in advancing knowledge on the domestic front. In her methodological protocol, Garcia asks for both multiculturalism and a return to ethnic studies, to promote justice and equality in the United States. The last category in her methodological protocol is *border consciousness*, which she takes from Gloria Anzaldua's text *Borderlands*. Anzaldua proposes the identity of a *mestiza*, which refers to a new form of identity and a new form of political proposal. This idea again resonates with the theme of the anthology; here, I cite the Indian proverb *bahate nadi and Ranate sadhu*, meaning that the river flows and wise men roam and extending the theme of border crossing. In this regard, it is interesting to see the way Garcia connects Anzaldua with Rosi Braidotti and her concept of nomadic subject.

The last piece in the volume is the poet-cum-philosopher Ifyani Menkiti's chapter, "Envisioning Global Citizenship," which directly addresses the theme of the anthology from a philosophical point of view. Menkiti engages with the discourses of two philosophers: the American philosopher John Rawls and Indian poet-cum-philosopher Rabindranath Tagore. In the fashion of a poet, he plunges into a quick discussion of Rawls's theory of global original position, for which Rawls has another term: "the second original position." I address Rawls's theory of the first original position and the veil of ignorance in my monograph *Negotiating Capability and Diaspora: A Philosophical Politics*; Rawls would override differences based on ethnicity, gender, and religion. Rawls proposes that we bypass these categories for the sake of political justice. Rawls's theory is a noble philosophy, but there are flaws, as Amartya Sen argues, because such an approach may erase the identity of a member of a minority group or a woman. Likewise, in the second original position or the global original position, Rawls's proposal that countries come together may result in our overlooking or bypassing the differences among people from various countries. Menkiti emphasizes that the theory of the global original position proposed by Rawls has been interpreted by scholars as a paradigm that overlooks people and asserts that we must foreground the cause of the people for camaraderie and peace. He therefore proposes the term *globalism*, which in Bengali is translated as *biswajaninata*, or universalism: we love others through ego-transcendence. Menkiti brings in the poet Tagore at the end of his piece, asserting the importance of achieving global peace through art forms or of achieving ego-transcendence through music, art, and poetry; his approach thereby resonates with that in my chapter, where I discuss Tagore's play *Red Oleanders* and the message of love, friendship, and dissolution of the master-slave dialectic. Menkiti observes, "Rabindranath Tagore was one of the writers who was fully aware of the importance of music and the arts in the civic and political lives of people. And the world is better for his wisdom—the world not just of Asia, but the world of the rest of us" (167).

I end with a quotation from my book *Humanitarian Identity and the Political Sublime:*

> Because we no longer live in a world guided by national boundaries, but we live in the transnational world—we live in the globe because the globe is a cosmic home now. . . . Thus, my theory is a multidimensional postcolonial feminist theory: I have two Indian male philosophers (Sri Aurobindo and Amartya Sen), beside all my feminist mentors and friends who empower me to articulate my own theory of the "political sublime" which we then can use to achieve a humanitarian identity, for a peaceful and transformed globe. I am not denying the West either; I also want to articulate emphatically that Kant's theory of the sublime to a certain extent intersects with my vision too. (134)

## BIBLIOGRAPHY

Aurobindo, Sri. 1997. *The Human Cycle, The Ideal of Human Unity, War and Self-determination*. Sri Aurobindo Ashram, Pondicherry, India: Sri Aurobindo Ashram Press (7th printing).

———. 1997, 2000. *The Future Poetry*. Sri Aurobindo Ashram, Pondicherry: Sri Aurobindo Ashram Publication Department.

Anzaldúa, Gloria. 1987. *Borderlands: The New Mestiza = La Frontera*. San Francisco: Spinsters/Aunt Lute.

Ashcroft, Bill, Gareth Griffith, and Helen Tiffin. 2005, 1989. *The Empire Writes Back*. London; New York: Routledge.

Appiah, Kwame Anthony. 1991. "Is the Post- in Postmodernism the Post- in Postcolonial?" *Critical Inquiry* 17: 336–357.

Barcelo, François. 1981. *La Tribu*, Montréal, Éditions Libre Expression.

Bhabha, Homi K. 1994. *The Location of Culture*. London and New York: Routledge.

Braidotti, Rosi. 1994. *Nomadic Subjects: Embodiment and Sexual Difference in Contemporary Feminist Theory*. New York: Columbia University Press.

Chomsky, Noam. June 6, 2013. Interview by Ashmita Khasnabish. *Author to Author Series*. Lexington, MA: LexMedia.

Das, Jagadish Chandra. 1969. *Akaser Papri* [in custody of Ashmita Khasnabish].

Devi, Ananda. 2007. "Bleu glace." In *Nouvelles de l'île Maurice*, 45–69. Paris: Magellan & Cie, coll. "Miniatures.'

Fanon, Frantz. 1967. *Black Skin, White Masks*. Translated by Charles Lam Markmann. New York: Grove Press.

García Márquez, Gabriel. 1970. *One Hundred Years of Solitude*, trans. Gregory Rabassa. New York: HarperCollins. [Traduction de *Cien años de soledad*, 1967.]

Hulme, Keri. 1985. *The Bone People*. Auckland/London: Spiral in association with Hodder and Stoughton.

———. 1986. *Te Kaihau/The Windeater*. Wellington: Victoria University Press.

Nye, Joseph. 2004. *Soft Power: The Means to Success in World Politics*. New York: Public Affairs.

Spivak, Gayatri. 1999. *A Critique of Postcolonial Reason: Toward a History of the Vanishing Present*. Cambridge, MA; London: Harvard University Press.

Said, W. Edward. 1979. *Orientalism*. New York: Vintage Books, Division of Random House.

Tagore, Rabindranath. 2010–2016. *Red Oleanders*. *In the Complete Works of Tagore*. Tagore-web.in.

*Chapter One*

# The Battle of Energy between Matter and Spirit

*Does It Direct Us to a Better Universe?*

Ashmita Khasnabish

One of the goals of my anthology is to find a solution to one of the many global problems that arises because as human beings we do not value each other. Thousands of years of history of human civilization has shown how human beings oppress each other and perpetuate the master-slave dialectic. It is very interesting as I ran into Albert Camus's book *Create Dangerously* in the Basil Blackwell Bookstore in Oxford last summer, which affirms the theme of my anthology that superficial friendship is not adequate. The main theme of this chapter is to explore if the conflict between matter and spirit[1] could be resolved. It is a tough nut to crack because it is difficult for civilization to fathom the truth that it is important to proceed in life with a significant amount of wisdom that we could derive from dealing with life but learning something out of life. But that learning does not take place without complete immersion in knowledge and culture of various races and we often forget that. Note the following quote from *Create Dangerously*:

> For I know as well as anyone the excess of intelligence, and I know as well as anyone that the intellectual is a dangerous animal ever ready to betray. But that is not the right kind of intelligence. We are speaking of the kind that is backed by courage, the kind that for four years paid what was necessary for the right to respect. When that intelligence is snuffed out, the black night of dictatorship begins. That is why we must maintain it with all its duties and all its rights. At that price, and only at that price, will French friendship have a meaning. For friendship is a knowledge acquired by free men. And there is no freedom without intelligence or without mutual understanding. (38)

13

The interesting part of the French-Algerian author's observation is that "friendship is a knowledge acquired by free men." It requires agreement with truth and mutual understanding. Camus's definition of friendship is rooted in fraternity and mutual understanding. It closely intersects on the one hand with the French Revolutions and on the other hand, with the Indian philosopher Sri Aurobindo's theory of the "Religion of Humanity" in *The Ideal of Human Unity*:

> Yet brotherhood is the real key to the triple gospel of the idea of humanity. The union of liberty and equality can only be achieved by the power of human brotherhood and it cannot be founded on anything else. But brotherhood exists only in the soul and by the soul and it exists by nothing else. . . . It is the practical recognition of this truth, it is the awakening of the soul in man and the attempt to get him to live from his soul and not from his ego which is the inner meaning of religion, and it is that to which the religion of humanity also must arrive before it can fulfill itself in the life of the race. (546–547)

What Camus calls the right kind of "intelligence," Sri Aurobindo renders as the "religion of humanity" and they seem to point to the similar direction—to the development of a nation attached to truth and comradery and feeling for each other rising from one's soul.

Thus, this chapter strives to construct a discourse looking into the future and reads the Indian Nobel Laureate Rabindranath Tagore's play *Red Oleanders* to explore what trajectory can lead us to the visionary dialogue so that we love each other as human beings as I articulated in my monograph *Humanitarian Identity and the Political Sublime: Intervention of a Postcolonial Feminist*, which I discuss a bit later.

Thus, the Bengali Nobel Laureate Tagore's drama *Raktakarabi* (*Red Oleanders*) on the one hand represents the core Indian philosophical theory as also represented in Sri Aurobindo's theory of the "Religion of Humanity" and on the other hand, resonates with Camus's theme and represents, unfolds, and dismantles what is called master-slave dialectic. The friendship that Camus is upholding referring to French friendship does constitute what we call according to Indian philosophy ego-transcendence, and it is achievable only when one learns the technique of mind-control. It has been explained in the ancient Indian philosophical text *Upanishad* many times and I would like to refer to the three different *Upanishads*. When Camus enunciates friendship he refers to it as a quality of mind that is not bound by any religion or politics but driven by the spirit or a liberated spirit. The liberation of the spirit can happen only when one can step out of their ego's boundary and connect to the world.

Mind control has several steps as explained by Sri Aurobindo in his book *The Life Divine*. According to that philosophy, "overmind consciousness" is a state of mind when one connects to the outside world but that connection has to be proper and just and without falsehood. In order to achieve that true consciousness or a state of mind without ego, one has to pass the following levels of mind: the journey starts at the level of higher mind and then there are illumined mind, intuition, and then overmind, and finally comes the supermind level of consciousness which is free of ego. It is reminiscent of the sloka from *Katha Upanishad*: "*Uttishthata jagrata prpya barannibodhota/ khurasya dhara nishita duratya durga pathasta kabayo badanti*" or "Awake, arise and learn by approaching the excellent ones. The path of knowledge is very sharp and steep as razor's edge (the wise ones describe that path to be as impassable as a razor's edge which once sharpened is difficult to tread on) poets inform us." This path is identical with what Camus mentions toward the end of the chapter "Defense Intelligence":

> I should like them not to give in when they are told that intelligence is always unwelcome or that it is permissible to lie in in order to succeed. I should like them not to give in to guile, to violence or to inertia. Then perhaps in a nation that is free and passionately attached to truth, man will begin again to have that feeling for man, without which the world can never be but vast solitude. (39)

What strikes me the most is the expression "man will begin again to have that feeling for man, without which the world can never be but vast solitude," which intersects with my theory of the "political sublime." Let me offer here a quote:

> So, in this book, I strove to sketch a philosophy which teaches us how we could live on the earth peacefully with each other as human beings focused on our humaneness and not primitive instinct, and this I also define as the "political sublime" where there is no difference between your pain and my pain; I as a human being share your pain, and you as a human being share mine. I love and respect you and you love and respect me and we do not compete and race as animals. (*Humanitarian Identity and the Political Sublime: Intervention of a Postcolonial Feminist* 2009, 133)

Compounded with this theme of intelligence comes the theme of freedom and artistic existence offered by Camus which resonates with the theme of *Raktakarabi*:

> It is not surprising that artists and intellectuals have been the first victim of modern tyrannies, whether of the right or of the left. Tyrants know there is in the work of art an emancipatory force, which is mysterious only to those who do not revere it. Every great work makes the human face more admirable and richer and this is its whole secret. And thousands of concentration camps and barred cells are not enough to hide this staggering testimony of dignity. . . . Yes, when modern tyranny shows us that, even when confined to his calling, the artist is a public enemy, it is right. But in this way tyranny pays its respects,

through the artist, to an image of man that nothing has ever been able to crush. (*Create Dangerously* 1958, 29–30)

At his lecture at Uppsala University in 1957, Camus states that art triumphs over everything and that in spite of all resistance artists should triumph: "And let us rejoice as artists, torn from our sleep and deafness, forced to keep our eyes on destitution, prisons and bloodshed." Tagore's symbolic play was composed in 1923, and it is amazing how both Nobel Laureates are vocalizing the claims of liberated men though the artist's voice of truth and emancipation. Both Nandini and Ranjan in the symbolic play *Raktakarabi* express their aspiration and urge for freedom from the slavery of matter and the so-called false King who represents false anarchy and power reducing human beings to numbers. Tagore calls this world of gross matter the Yaksha Town and in order to understand the complete philosophical underpinning, one needs to delve into Indian philosophy. It says in the *Isha Upanishad*: "*Hiranmayen patren satyasa apihitam mukham; tat tang pushana apabrinu, satya dharmaaa dishtaye*" or "The face of truth is covered by the golden lid: O Sun-God please, open the lid so that we can see the truth." When in his Upanishadic mantra, the golden lid is comparable to gross matter and Sun-God is invoked to dismantle that material shield, in the play, Nandini is given the task to break that shield of gold nuggets which create unnecessary and unwanted pressure in human life. The professor in the play explains to Nandini, "In this Yaksha town all our treasure is of gold, the secret treasure of the dust. But the gold which represents you, beautiful one, is not of the dust, but the light which never owns any bond" (*Raktakarabi*). The professor who seems to play a choric voice genuinely appreciates Nandini and her liberated spirit and is aware of the binding of the matter and material world in the Yaksha town. But strangely enough, his role is limited or constrained as he cannot do much to accelerate the process of liberation. The professor is trapped in the world of matter and so badly trapped that he along with other diggers thinks of himself as insects in a hole in the laborious toil and Nandini as an evening star representing leisure. Let us hear the conversation between Nandini and the professor:

> Professor: Do you know Nandini, I too live behind a network of scholarship. I am an unmitigated scholar, just as our king is an unmitigated king.
>
> Nandini: You are laughing at me, Professor. But tell me, when they brought me here, why didn't they bring my Ranjan also?
>
> Professor: It's their way to snatch things by fractions. But why should you want to drag your life's treasure down amongst this dead wealth of ours?
>
> Nandini: Because I know he can put a beating heart behind these dead ribs.

Professor: Your own presence is puzzling enough for our governors here; if Ranjan also comes they will be in despair. . . .

Nandini: My Ranjan's strength is like that of your river, Sankhini, it can laugh and yet it can break. . . . I shall meet Ranjan today. (*Red Oleanders* in Tagoreweb.in 2010–2016, 5)

In this encounter between the professor and Nandini we note again the resistance of matter to spirit. One could notice the expressions: "dead wealth," "dead ribs," "stones," "gross muscles" and contrast these expressions with Nandini's expressions: "beating heart," "God's own laughter," "strength is like that of your river, Sankhini, it can laugh and yet it can break." And a little further down in the play the professor is harping on the truth that the Yaksha town is a city under collapse and the territory of the Shadow Demon who lives in the gold cave. The reason that Ranjan has not been brought into this dark pit of the Shadow Demon and gold cave are that he belongs to light and laughter. One could go back again to the sloka from the *Upanishad* that the face of truth is covered by the golden lid and as human beings we pray to uncover that lid to see the truth and the prayer is being offered to Sun-God. Golden lid here stands for the material or dead wealth that is being discussed in *Red Oleanders*. Ranjan represents light, divine laughter, and the energy of the river Sankhini. Ranjan also represents nature and the flower Red Oleanders, which in Bengali is called "Raktakarabi." Even the professor is asking Nandini why she is decorating herself with Red Oleanders and whether the color red indicates any bad omen, but she explains that Ranjan likes Red Oleanders and calls her Red Oleanders and she wears it on her neck, on her breast, and on her arms.

Although, there is an omen lurking in it because eventually Ranjan has to be sacrificed in this battle between matter and spirit. The sacrifice of Ranjan reminds me of Camus's observation: "One may long for a gentler flame, a respite, a pause from musing. But perhaps there is no other peace for the artist than what he finds in the combat" (Camus 1950, 32). Nandini as a representative of the art world has to undertake that fight not just with the professor, but with the king himself who represents absolute monarchy, capitalism, bad power, and everything negative and associated with stark matter as we can note expressed in Nandini's question of the king: "Are you not afraid, king, of handling the dead wealth of the earth?" (Tagoreweb.in 2010–2016, 5). So, again the tussle is between the live nature and dead matter. But the king is too domineering and when Nandini asks him to come out in the open light and not to stay beneath the earth and torture her by digging gold, he answers in his bleak manner. He compares his hiding with Nandini's mystical presence—that it is hard to fathom Nandini's beauty too and he would rather clench and crush that beauty in his closed fist or break her into pieces. This is just the mere howling of a greedy king who further demands to crush the red oleanders worn by Nandini and build a dream. He cries in frustration, "Those few frail petals guard it and hinder me. Within you there is the same hindrance, so strong because so soft. Nandini, will you tell me what you think of me?"

The next phase of the drama is intriguing as the king calculates by himself that his dance rhythm is different than Nandini's. It seems that the king is on the way to his realization that how power destroys itself is by its own weight. Power is self-destructive. His next observation is more spirted as he alludes to rhythm and cosmic harmony and narrates that rhythm, or as it says in Bengali *tal* or chanda, is attuned to the harmony that pervades in the sky and connects stars and planets and it enlightens the burden of matter. Much later in the play the king also gives the example of the frog that was trapped in the well for three thousand years and the king crushes it and saves it that way. This metaphor is associated with the common Indian proverb of being a *kupamanduk*, one who stays in the well and very narrow-minded. Nandini compares it with stone walls which will be shattered soon as she will meet Ranjan. The king screams that if Nandini had adorned the king with red oleanders, he would have died in peace. But observe the dialogue between the king and Nandini as the king wants to kill Ranjan:

> Nandini: Someone loves red oleanders and calls me in that name. It is in remembrance of him that I wear these flowers.
>
> Voice: Then, I tell you, they're going to be his evil start as well as mine.
>
> Nandini: Don't say such things for shame! I am going.
>
> Voice: Where?
>
> Nandini: When Ranjan comes he'll see I am waiting for him. . . .
>
> Voice: I should tread hard on Ranjan and grind him in the dust. (Tagoreweb.in 2010–2016, 20)

What is missing is what Sri Aurobindo said: "Brotherhood exists in the soul and by the soul and exists by nothing else." The king is devoid of any sense of brotherhood. That is what Camus said is the true form of intelligence and that is why we have all the bad consequences like holocaust, partition, and now the refugee crisis. The king represents that capitalistic power and that totalitarian power which crush all harmony and happiness in the universe. Let us hear the stanza from *Savitri* interpreted by Jagadish Chandra Das:

Yearning for the straight paths of eternity
And from their high station looked down on this world
Two sun-gaze Daemons witnessing all that is. (*Savitri* 1940, 258)

The poet/philosopher that I am alluding to interprets this stanza very well; he interprets the word "Daemon" going to its Greek roots where it serves to signify a connection between the terrestrial and the extra-terrestrial worlds. Let me offer here a translation of the author's interpretation: "Daemon means 'A Spirit holding a middle place, between gods and man, and it is defined as the genius of Socrates.'"[2] What is Nandini's role in the play *Red Oleanders*? It seems Nandini works as a Dameon or a connecting Spirit between the King and Ranjan; the King representing bad materialistic energy dammed up in Yaksha Town through nuggets of gold where the laborers are called by numbers and anybody who wants to break the net woven by the king gets opposition. One such character is Bishnu who is the allay of Nandini. Bishnu's articulation clarifies the matter more: "Ever since coming to Yaksha Town the sky has dropped out of my life. I felt as if they had pounded me in the same mortar with all the fractions of men here. Then you came and looked into my face in a way that made me sure some light could still be seen through me" (5)! "Yes, you are my messenger from the unreachable shore" (6)! Through a mystic song of Bishnu, sorrow is conveyed beautifully: "*Ogo dukhjagania tomay gan sonab: o-go ghumbhngnia tomay gan sonab*" ("O the waker of sleep I will sing for you: o the waker of grief I will sing for you"). Nandini is that harbinger and let us encounter Ranjan though Nandini:

> No, he holds an oar in each hand and ferries me across the stormy waters; he catches wild horses by the mane and rides with me through the woods. As he jumps into the Nagai river and disturbs its current with his joyous splashing, so he disturbs me with his tumultuous life. Desperately he stakes his all on the game and thus has he won me. You also were there with us, but you held aloof, and at last something urged you one day to leave our gambling set. (Tagoreweb.in 2010–2016, 16)

Although Nandini uses the term "gambling set" she refers to the cosmic play of "jouissance" and "ego-transcendence." What is "jouissance" and what is "ego-transcendence"? For that I have to fall back on my monograph *Jouissance as Ananda: Indian Philosophy, Feminist Theory and Literature*, and especially to the chapter "Jouissance as Ananda: Bliss." "Jouissance" is a French psychoanalytical term used by Jacques Lacan, which created a lot of repercussions among the French feminists. The feminist who inveighed against it most strongly was Luce Irigaray because she challenged the binary division between the imaginary and the symbolic orders, according to which women are subordinate and associated with the imaginary order which basically is the unconscious.[3] Luce Irigaray absolved the term "jouissance" from the shackle of Western psychoanalysis and reconfigured jouissance as women's jouissance as well as inscribing it as strength ranging from the corporeal to the celestial. But I added one more step to the theory of jouissance via the Indian philosophical term *"ananda,"* which means "bliss," and one could achieve that through the process of ego-transcendence. According to Sigmund Freud, the ego is the supreme level of consciousness but according to both ancient and modern Indian philosophy, one has to go beyond ego to achieve that, and both Tagore and Sri Aurobindo advocate for that. The subtle difference between these two philosophers resides in the fact that Tagore perceives ego-transcendence occurring thorough songs and poetry which are based on ancient Upanishadic philosophy. Sri Aurobindo based his own philosophy of "supramental consciousness" on Upanishadic philosophy by which different levels of mind range from the higher mind to supermind and as such could be considered as a psychoanalytical theory.

What is most important in Nandini's observation is the concept of game: she was engaged in the game with Ranjan who is tumultuous and ecstatic and jumps into the tumultuous river. He risks everything for game? So, what is this game? This game could be conceived as a game where you engage a free spirit devoid of ego and materialistic greed. It is a game which could be inscribed as both "jouissance" and *"ananda"* achievable though transcending ego. Thus, Nandini not only plays the role of Daemon as a link between earth and heaven but also as a symbol of jouissance and ego-transcendence and Bishnu and Kishor are her allies. However, there is an impediment to jouissance and Ranjan's death manifests that limitation of human goodwill. That Ranjan has to die for the King to realize the ultimate truth is proof that the world is inundated by problems that range from the Holocaust to the partition of Indian, from colonization to slavery and racism—to name it whatever you want—encompassing all sorts of torture human beings can inflict on each other in a shameless manner.

To mitigate that problem, I theorized through my theory of jouissance as ananda and ego-transcendence, and the theory of the "political sublime" in a neo-Kantian way defining my identity as a postcolonial feminist, but the question is, where we go from here? Homi Bhabha addresses his commitment to theory by very convincingly interrogating Western paradigms in *The Location of Culture* and poststructuralism, among other isms. But one caveat against him is that he is catering to Western paradigms by rejecting the idea of a solution in terms of transcendence, which he also calls sublation. Here one could think of Toni Morrison's *Beloved* where the ghost triumphs through being resurrected. I discussed in great detail in my chapter on *Beloved* in *Negotiating Capability and Diaspora* the concept of sublimation of pain achieved through the return of Beloved. The return of Beloved is comparable to Satyvan's return from death in Sri Aurobindo's epic *Savitri*. Let me offer the quote here:

The return to earth and resurrection of Satyavan's body from the clutch of Death is similar to the resurrection of Morrison's Beloved—with the distinction that Beloved brings herself back from the underworld by her own willpower and effort, whereas Savitri as a wife brings back Satyavan to life; the theory of love and marriage enters the discourse of resurrection here. However, the common theme is the resurrection and embodiment of spirit. The closest replica we find in modern American philosophy is in Quine's theory which collapses the dualstic mind-body divide. . . . But my concern here is not so much to resolve the philosophical problem of the mind-body dualism but to propose and assert that what was achieved by Morrison in the resurrection of the character of Beloved is highly philosophical both in the Eastern/Indian and Western philosophical ways. At the end of the book Beloved acquires an identity which is both material and abstract. (*Negotiating Capability and Diaspora: A Philosophical Politics* 2013, 133)

We need more Beloveds to be born so we join the earth with the sky and reduce the distance between matter and spirit. Beloved is like Nandini in *Red Oleanders*: the professor articulates how Nandini could bridge the sky with the earth. The professor tells Nandini to gaze upward because flowers bloom upward, although the roots of the tree go underneath the ground. "The tree spreads its root fingers and does its grabbing underground, but there it does not bring forth its flowers. Flowers bloom on the branches which reach towards the light" (Tagoreweb.in 2010, 28). Both the planes are necessary: the earth and the light of heaven which are accessible through flowers which reach toward light. Let us analyze one more time Homi Bhabha's observation: "When I talk of negotiation rather than negation, it is to convey a temporality that makes it possible to conceive of the articulation of antagonistic or artistic elements: a dialectic without the emergence of a teleological or transcendent History" (*The Location of Culture* 1994, 37). He insists that he does not want the redemptive rationality or sublation or transcendence and that is not a form of negotiation for him. This is an excellent comment but the question remains about the meaning of the word or the interpretation of the word "negotiation." The word "negotiation" as I understand it, stands not just for understanding or articulating differences or opinions of different groups, but there must be a gesture or nuance for mediation and if not a complete solution, then a progress or a compromise between different viewpoints. I do not agree with Bhabha that the task of negotiation ends with a mere quarrel. I am delighted that he established "theory" as the ground for struggle, but mere struggle cannot lead us anywhere. However, I like his following observation: "From the perspective of negotiation and translation, contra Franz Fanon and Jean-Paul Sartre there can be no final discursive closure of theory. The corollary is that there is no first or final act of revolutionary social (or socialist) transformation" (*The Location of Culture* 1994, 45). What is so plausible in this observation is Bhabha's invocation of the sense of infinity in the Derri-

dean sense, which is rather metaphysical. Bhabha acknowledges the notion
of infinity and ongoing-ness and believes firmly that there can be no final
stage of revolutionary social or socialist transformation. He does not believe
in foreclosure of political battles. Here I notice Bhabha contradicting himself
and taking his cue I go to the next stage of argumentation.

In my monograph *Negotiating Capability and Diaspora: A Philosophical
Politics*, I offer negotiation but I interpret it as a tool to negotiate one's
identity and existence and negotiating with a certain form of theory. I bring
in a dialogue between the American philosopher John Rawls's theory of
justice and primary goods with Amartya Sen's theory of capability. In the
Bhabhavian way, the theory of "capability" arose as a critique of John
Rawls's theory: whereas John Rawls offers his theory of the "original positions" and asks people of different ethnicities, religions, etc. to bypass the
differences and come to an agreement for the sake of political justice, and
defines this as the first Original Position, where he seeks to resolve problems
of society by bringing the two terms "comprehensive doctrines" and "political justice" together, "comprehensive doctrines" holding differences under
that umbrella and political justice as a norm, Sen critiques this structure by
being afraid of erasure of differences. Thus his theory of capability emerges
as a critique of Rawls's theory asking for exposing the differences between
the powerful and powerless strata of human society and also cultivating
willpower in terms of "capability," which he calls "reason to value." The
point I am trying to make is that theory has great potential for this never-
ending journey of knowledge making and we should not deny ourselves that
privilege. Bhabha will agree with me on this but the question arises with
what I do with the next part of my theory. I offer a solution with the next part
of my theory: I suggested that we could bring philosophers together and
come to a compromise. In that dialogue, I brought the East with the West and
brought the materialists and the idealist philosophers together.

So, my point is that I am seeking a solution for the problem that occurs
through discrimination and one party looking down upon the other. If one
looks through history, one could find many such moments of discrimination,
which are beyond my reach of knowledge as a singular human being, and I
am presenting here one poem translated by myself to offer you an example of
one of these moments. The poet writes (I am translating):

> Why cannot I unite the earth and the sky?
> The more the sky becomes wide
> The earth shrinks and your relatives get lost.
> In the coal mine.
> Just like the laborers of the coal mine of Ratibari (a specific place the poet is
> referring to)
> Being underground-locked for one hundred and twenty-five hours in darkness

******

My sisters, villagers, relatives, neighbors of my country
They are also imprisoned within the cave of Pakistan
They did not die, but sucked in the life of death before death
One day death will come, but did not yet, their hope did not die, did not get
extinguished. (Jagadish Chandra Das, unpublished manuscript)

This poem with its intense tone reminds me of Sashi Tharoor's speech on "Britain Owes Reparations to India." The poem is set up in the context of the Partition of India: you can see in the poem excruciating pain inscribed through the imagery of the coal mine. Partition caused the separation between the poet and his family and he mourns it. The poet is looking at this situation in the year 1969, three years prior to the independence of East Pakistan from Pakistan. But the Partition caused the separation which caused the poet immense grief and Sashi Tharoor in his glorious speech points it out clearly and strongly.

What shocked me most was the economic deprivation triggered by the British colonization: one of the prominent examples is the famine which killed 40 million people and the other one is that the British owed 200 million pounds to India from World War II, among other atrocities including making Indian weavers poor. The poet's grief that the earth and the sky can never touch each other is very significant and so are the lines "My sisters, villagers, relatives, neighbors of my country/They are also imprisoned within the cave of Pakistan/They did not die, but sucked in the life of death before death." Sashi Tharoor chalks out very well all the atrocities committed to Indians and that the British owe a moral debt to the Indians. They did give reparations to the Maoris of New Zealand, and why not to the Indians of India? Tharoor offers me this sharp line with the pungent tone: "to oppress, maim, enslave, kill people for two hundred years and then say you are democratic."

In Tharoor's voice and also in the poet's voice we hear a tone of despair as well as hope. It is not exactly just protest but protest compounded with a note of future vision: the poet says that "one day death will come, but did not yet, their hope did not die, did not get extinguished." Tharoor very strongly and logically claims at the end of his speech that for the next two hundred years 1 pound each day must be paid to Indians by the British as a moral debt. In it I see a note of solution and a future trajectory, as does the poet reveal at the end of his poem: "Their hope did not die, did not get extinguished." It is almost a prophetic comment because three years later, in 1971, East Pakistan became liberated from Pakistan. I want to bring in Bishnu of *Red Oleanders* again in the discussion: when Nandini is shocked to see how Bishnu is treated with the marks of flogging and he comments, "They have a big beast inside them, that's why their heads are not lowered by the indignity of man" (31). One may ask the question whether Tagore who was writing at the British Colonial time is alluding to the British oppressor through the personality of the egoistic King whose voice we have heard so far and not a real presence and his accomplices who apparently treated Bishnu so viciously.

Now let us see the confrontation between Nandini and the king: the King destroys or kills Ranjan who represents life. The struggle between Nandini and Ranjan represents the eternal conflict between matter and spirit, between the oppressor and the oppressed, between the center and the margin, and the list goes on and on. Nandini knocks at the door of the king; notice their encounter and conversation:

> Voice: You want Ranjan, I know. I have asked the Governor to fetch him at once. But don't remain standing at the door.
>
> . . .
>
> Voice: Today is for the Flag-worship. Don't distract my mind. Get away from my door.
>
> Nandini: The gods have all eternity for their worship. They're not pressed for time. But the sorrows of men cannot wait.
>
> King: Deceive! These traitors have deceived me, perdition take them! My own machine refuses my sway!
>
> Nandini: King, they all say you know magic. Make him wake up for my sake.
>
> King: My magic can only put an end to waking. Alas! I know not how to awaken. (38)

Here the pain of Nandini, the poet suffering from the partition, and Sashi Tharoor's articulation of maiming, killing, enslaving get merged together. I echo here again what I said in the *Humanitarian Identity and the Political Sublime*: "Because we no longer live in a world divided by national boundaries, but we live in the transnational world—we live in a globe because the globe is a cosmic home now. But still why we do have war and not peace on the earth? Why do we need war to control human beings?" In order to resolve that crisis of humanity, I have recourse to this philosophical discourse offered in the form of the symbolic play *Red Oleanders*, or *Raktakarabi*. In Nandini's cry of agony, I hear the intense pain of the poet articulated: "King, they all say you know magic. Make him wake up for my sake." But the King does not know how to awaken and he confesses that he knows how to put everything to death.

The king here resembles the King of Death Yama of Hindu mythology and Sri Aurobindo, the Indian philosopher in his hyper-epic *Savitri*, where Yama argues with Savitri that her husband cannot be brought back to life. I have to refer to the chapter "Savitri and the Political Sublime" of *Humanitarian Identity and the Political Sublime: Intervention of a Postcolonial Feminist*. In Book 10, "Double Twilight," Canto 3, "The Debate of Love and Death," the god of Death poses challenges and discouragements to Savitri, asking her to return to earth without Satyvan: "Return, O child, to thy forsaken earth." Death carries on its battle with Savitri, portraying the world as a place of imperfection and falsehood: "But here are only facts and steel-bound Law. This truth I know that Satyavan is dead. . . . No magic truth can bring the dead to life" (25)! This debate represents in a nutshell what the Indian philosopher Sri Aurobindo develops as the metaphysical battle between matter and spirit, or between reason and spirit, as I observed: "The debate between Yama the god of Death and Savitri is crucial to understand the battle between matter/reason and spirit in Sri Aurobindo's phenomenology" (125). So, where does Savitri intersect with the cry of Nandini? Savitri defeats Yama and brings Satyavan back to life: but Nandini joins Ranjan in death and here death is identical with freedom from oppression or it could be interpreted as the sacrifice of the artist from oppression or bourgeoisie.

I want to conclude talking about the French philosopher Jean Wahl who is not that popular in the United States because of his connection with theology, as I learned reading Levinas's letter. But as a matter of fact, he is the father figure and mentor to many or all modern French philosophers from Jacques Derrida to Gilles Deleuze. I am profoundly interested in his philosophy because he shares the same beliefs I have as an Indian feminist philosopher. Following Georg Wilhelm Friedrich Hegel's phenomenology of consciousness, he interprets unhappy consciousness, which I call discontentment, as something which would work toward the happy consciousness, or my terms *contentment* and *fulfillment*. He also brings in the third angle or unity where the unhappy consciousness merges into happy consciousness. Let us here turn to Jean Wahl's quote, "What he calls the triplicity of concept or the glimpse of the unity of duality" strongly intersects with Indian philosophy which believed in the dissolution of binary division between matter and spirit. Wahl claims in his book that it is grounded in Christian philosophy, but it is the root of Indian philosophy as well. The reason I have recourse to Wahl as well to interpret my philosophy is that I believe in optimism and solution in spite of the bleakness of the world. I believe that matter and spirit binary would be dissolved through approaching transcendence and bringing transcendence to immanence. Transcendence does not have to be an abstract phenomenon, but a purified state of mind which I call political sublime or a philosophical politics. If we could achieve that benign state of mind even through the song of Bishnu or the philosophy of true friendship of Camus, we could solve the problems of the world. Orient should be valorized but in that valorization we could adore some of the Western theories that are not grossly bound to reason.

## NOTES

1. The matter-spirit battle is almost a battle between the East and the West or the Global North or the Global South. In this chapter, I strove to bring them together negotiating about both globalization and diaspora and harping on the theme of universal love and humanism.

2. I quote and use this notion of Daemon as used by the poet as highly significant, because it alludes to the connection between the heaven and the earth, or the connection between immanence and transcendence, which has been valorized in Greek philosophy, Indian philosophy, and by a few Western philosophers like Jean Wahl and Henry Bergson and Walter Benjamin, among others.

3. She reread the term as adding a celestial dimension to it: "I valorize Irigaray's theory of jouissance because it incorporated the sublime dimension and as such advanced beyond the limitations of Western psychoanalytical theories of Freud and Lacan. Still it needs to address what happens when women are established in the symbolic plane, but it does not address to the full extent the dissolution of the ego, which I try to resolve by introducing an Indian psychoanalytical/philosophical context" (4).

## BIBLIOGRAPHY

Aurobindo, Sri. 1950, 1993. *Savitri: A Legend and a Symbol*. Pondicherry, India: Sri Aurobindo Ashram Publication Department.
———. 1997. *The Human Cycle, The Ideal of Human Unity, War and Self-determination*. Sri Aurobindo Ashram, Pondicherry, India: Sri Aurobindo Ashram Press (7th printing).
Bhabha, Homi K. 1994. *The Location of Culture*. London and New York: Routledge.
Camus, Albert. 1950, 1953, 1958. UK: Penguin Random House.
Das, Jagadish Chandra. 1972. *Savitri, A Series of Lectures*. Calcutta, India: Associated Publishing Company.
———. 1969. *Akaser Papri* [in custody of Ashmita Khasnabish].
Khasnabish, Ashmita. 2009. *Humanitarian Identity and the Political Sublime*. Lanham, Boulder, New York, Toronto, Plymouth, UK: Lexington Books, Rowman & Littlefield Publishing Group.
———. 2014, 2016. *Negotiating Capability and Diaspora: A Philosophical Politics*. Lanham, Boulder, New York, Toronto, Plymouth, UK: Lexington Books, Rowman & Littlefield Publishing Group.
Tagore, Rabindranath. 2010–2016. *Red Oleanders. In the Complete Works of Tagore*. Tagoreweb.in.
Wahl, Jean. 2017. *Transcendence and the Concrete: Selected Writings*. Fordham University Press.

*Chapter Two*

# After Neoliberalism and Post-structuralism

*Postcolonial Studies, Diaspora, and Globalization*

## Paget Henry

The insurgent anti-colonial struggles of the twentieth century gave rise to a new and third round of projects of postcolonial nation building. The first round of these struggles against European imperialism took root in the eighteenth century with revolutions in Haiti and the North American colonies against French and British colonial rule. In the nineteenth century, we had the Latin American revolutions against Spanish and Portuguese colonial rule. Both of these earlier rounds of revolutionary uprisings gave birth to projects of postcolonial nation building with widely varying outcomes. Thus it is that the anti-colonial struggles of the twentieth century constituted a third set of revolutionary attempts at ending European imperial domination—this time in the regions of Africa, Asia, the Caribbean and the Middle East.

This third set of anti-colonial struggles was inspired and guided by an equally insurgent set of texts among which we can note those by Gandhi, Aurobindo, Garvey, W. E. B. Du Bois, Claudia Jones, Frantz Fanon, Kwame Nkrumah, and Gamal Nasser. These were revolutionary texts, which called upon the colonized to rise up, to throw off the imperial, racial, class and gender chains by which they were bound, and to build for ourselves strong and free nations that would be alternatives to those of the West.

With the gaining of political independence, between the 1940s and the 1980s, by the colonized territories of Africa, Asia, the Caribbean and the Middle East, this third round of postcolonial nation building began. With great enthusiasm and high expectations the new leaders and people of these countries began various journeys into the postcolonial era. Filled with the

27

confidence from our efforts at rolling back the boundaries of European empires, and disregarding the experiences of the nations of the first and second rounds of uprisings, we expected to see major transformations in the colonial structures of our societies in our lifetime. In the Caribbean, it was to the rhythms and harmonies of the calypsos and the steel bands that we began our journey into the postcolonial era.

However, as the stubborn realities of our situation began to sink in, the pleasant sounds of our postcolonial euphoria soon turned quite dissonant. With the departure of this early euphoria, it was the reality of neocolonialism that became visible. This phenomenon had been ably theorized for us by the then leader of Ghana, Kwame Nkrumah who, like Patrice Lamumba of the Congo, would soon be overthrown by a Western-inspired coup. This focus on neocolonialism marked an important shift in Nkrumah's earlier position, when he advised the colonized to seek first the political kingdom and all things would be added unto you. This heightened awareness of neocolonialism brought home the extent to which the economies of this third group of postcolonial countries were still externally owned and that this pattern of imperial ownership would only increase in the "postcolonial" era. Further, this confrontation with neocolonialism as the imperial shadow haunting our postcolonial present also made it clear that our "independent states" were still subject to constraints rooted in the strategic and geopolitical interests of the imperial nations.

As these counter-revolutionary trends continued to mature and gain strength, the Caribbean started moving to music with a different beat. Receding into the background were lilting and expectant rhythms of the calypso and along with them the earlier theories of rapid economic development. Their places were being taken by the more dissonant ideas and sounds of dependency theory, reggae, dancehall, soca and reggaetone. By the mid-1970s, these disturbing sounds and ideas of neocolonial trouble only got louder, triggering great debates over who was to blame, which set of policies or what practices of corruption was responsible for the crisis in our project of nation building.

Adding to this rising drama, the major Western powers were coming to the end of a period of Keynesian-inspired growth and entering into an era of crisis as our neocolonial troubles were continuing to mount. The postwar boom in the Western economies had also unleashed a number of student-led insurrectionary social movements that we can mark here by the year 1968. The end of the decade of the 1970s, as the Western boom continued to morph into a stagflation crisis, saw the containing of these forces for change by the economic and political directorates of the postwar social order. This project of counter-revolutionary containment changed attitudes toward radical social change in both the West and our post/neocolonial world. Out of the disappointments and clashes of opposing ideas and policies produced by this peri-

od of dual crisis, there emerged new theoretical discourses that would dominate the reading and policy responses to the crisis that had overtaken this
third round of postcolonial nation building. These were of course the discourses of neoliberalism and post-structuralism.

This chapter will argue that the rise to epistemic power of these discourses constituted a form of hegemonic capture as they came to occupy the
founding centers of economic and critical thinking in many postcolonial
societies. It will further argue that, with both now in decline, it is vital that
we re-establish ourselves at the centers of postcolonial economic and critical
thinking.

## NEOLIBERALISM, NEOCOLONIALISM, AND HEGEMONIC CAPTURE

Neoliberalism was a return to the liberal economic and trading policies of the
1890s, which were spearheaded by Britain and collapsed in 1914 with the
start of the First World War. Neoliberalism was therefore a rejection of the
state interventionist policies of John Maynard Keynes, which eventually got
the Western economies over the collapse of 1914. These market-centered
approaches to economic theory and practice were seen as the solution to the
crises of both the Western and the postcolonial economies. With regard to the
crises of the postcolonial economies, one of the primary results of this neoliberal turn was the reinforcing of the neocolonialism of the postcolonial
period through the further extending of Western imperial ownership and
control of the economies of these ex-colonial societies. At the discursive
level, the imposing of these policies resulted in a hegemonic re-capturing of
the direction of economic thinking and a re-asserting of the colonial view of
these postcolonial economies as formations that are without growth engines
unless they functioned as extensions of European and American economies.

In 1885, John Stuart Mill gave one of the classic statements of this colonial view of these now postcolonial economies: "These are hardly to be looked
upon as countries, carrying on an exchange of commodities with other countries, but more properly as outlying agricultural or manufacturing establish-
ments belonging to larger communities. . . . Our West India colonies, for
example, cannot be regarded as countries with a productive capital of their
own" (2008:65). In other words, just as the colonial view asserted that we
had no capacity for philosophical production, with greater power to back it
up this view also asserted that we were without the capacity to generate and
sustain a productive capital of our own. The insurgent economic ideas and
practices of the 1950s, 1960s, and 1970s, which we can mark here by the
UNCTAD's proposals for a New International Economic Order (NIEO), was
a direct challenge to this view of entrepreneurship in formerly colonized

territories. This was one of the primary goals of the work of economists like Raul Prebisch, Carlos Diaz Alejandro, Arthur Lewis, George Beckford, Clive Thomas, and Samir Amin.

Neoliberalism revived the above colonial view and transformed it into a neocolonial one in which postcolonial economies were still seen as peripheral extensions of Western economies. This was very clear in the new foreign capital and export-driven models of growth and crisis resolution that were pushed by the IMF and the World Bank, particularly after the de-industrialization of major Western economies and their subsequent financialization. Gone completely were insurgent projects of owning and controlling the commanding heights of our own economies via new models of state and local private sector cooperation, and the more institutional economic thinking behind them. Replacing them were projects of reducing the role of the state, re-creating what we used to call a "comprador local bourgeoisie," and legitimating all of these changes was the new market-centered economic thinking of Milton Friedman, Friedrich Hayek and others. One of the major Caribbean markers of this hegemonic capture was the turning of the Prime Minister of Jamaica, Michael Manley, and social theorists like Don Robotham to neoliberal policies after being such visible leaders of the democratic socialist alternative in the region. For a while, Robotham was an advocate of the ideas of Jeffrey Sachs as a basis for restructuring the Jamaican economy.

Thus, in addition to being a case of the external imposition of an economic discourse by powerful organizations of Western imperial rule, the ascendance of neoliberalism was also a battle for space between a dependent institutional and a market approach to economic theory and practice. It was a battle between states, markets and supporting institutions at the founding center of economic discourse. In this battle, indigenous traditions of economic theory and practice were de-centered and replaced. This decentering and replacing was not the result of an extended debate in which evidence and the better arguments were clearly on the side of neoliberalism. Rather the outcome was the result of the more rapid maturing of the crises of the postcolonial economies than those of the Western economies. By the early 1980s, around 70 highly indebted postcolonial countries were knocking on the door of the IMF seeking finance to cover trade deficits and rising debt payments. It was in these vulnerable positions that most of these countries had neoliberal policies imposed on them. As a result, we soon had "experts" in Washington setting targets and conditionalities for the liberalization and privatization of postcolonial economies in exchange for needed finance, which had to be paid back with interest. It was under the short-term pressure of these financial arrangements that local projects of longer-term economic development and independence were abandoned.

As a result, this was a very visible and public hegemonic capturing of the discourses on the 1970s crises of the postcolonial economies. These crises were no longer seen as neocolonial in nature but the result of excessive state intervention, the inability of local private sector initiative to generate a sustained growth dynamic, corruption or some combination of these factors. Consequently, policies of privatizing state enterprises, weakening of trade unions, transforming of labor and democratic socialist parties into liberal ones, and implementing a variety of austerity programs came to dominate the policy arena over the last three and a half decades. Adding to the high costs of this hegemonic capture were the highly negative results of these neoliberal policies for most of these postcolonial economies. They certainly have not given to these economies the growth engines they are supposedly lacking.

In short, one of the major outcomes of this period of neoliberal capture has been a strong reinforcing of the long-established and self-interested Western view of postcolonial economic performance that systematically rejects the oppositional elements in postcolonial economic thinking and distorts its developmental practices. The distorting effect of this imperial/IMF view can be seen in the sharp decline in original postcolonial economic thinking that has come with this extended period of hegemonic capture. Further, as in earlier colonial periods, this neoliberal era has inhibited and systematically undervalued the entrepreneurial capabilities of postcolonial states and private sector entrepreneurs to respond constructively to local economic challenges. Thus the support and cooperation that local economists and political and business leaders have given to the demands of the neoliberal order have been major contributors of the increasing neocolonial features of our postcolonial present, and to the decline of the insurgent economic alternatives that marked the start of this present era.

## POST-STRUCTURALISM, NEOCOLONIALISM, AND HEGEMONIC CAPTURE

If neoliberalism captured the imagination of economic elites in the postcolonial societies, then it was the critical imagination of their cultural elites that was captured by post-structuralism. This French discourse offered a new or deconstructive style of critique that many diasporic postcolonial scholars would deploy in the interest of understanding the crises that had overtaken their home societies. What was new in post-structuralism was the re-ordering of the key binary oppositions assumed by the main tradition of Western metaphysics, which resulted in an inverting of the old primacy of speech over writing. This establishing of the primacy of writing over speech, and over just about everything else, produced a new philosophy of language that would ground the practices of deconstructive critique.

In the case of Jacques Derrida, the inverting of this binary was the surface manifestation of a deeper "rupture" (1978:278) in our thinking about centered epistemic structures. This rupture promised a revolution in how we thought about discursive centers that generated such structures, and about the metaphysics by which they legitimated their claims as centers. Thus it was the very "structurality of structure" that was at stake in Derrida's approach to discursive centers and their correlated metaphysics (1978:279). Indeed another primary goal of his deconstructive practice was to show that the reason employed by Western metaphysics made extensive use of the figurative and metaphorical language that it categorically rejects. Derrida further suggested that these figurative and metaphorical strategies are themselves rooted in a deeper stratum of arche-writing. The latter is the creative work of what Derrida called "differance"—the fundamental activity of sequencing the matter or material being of language in time and space, of differing and deferring that is the *a priori* condition for all linguistic activity including meaningful everyday speaking and writing (1978:293). Differance would be a new kind of center, one that would hopefully escape the metaphysical entanglements of earlier centers such as God, essence, consciousness, etc.

As in the case of neoliberalism, the rise of post-structuralism was also the result of a theoretical battle between local institutionally grounded creole, nationalist, religious and other responses to the crisis, and this semio-linguistically grounded approach to critiquing established discourses offered by post-structuralism. Whatever was the *a priori* center or ground of these creole, nationalist, religious and other discourses, it would now have to make major room for the presence of arche-writing and its play of differance. In whatever the fashion, this movement of differance would now have to be at the center of things postcolonial.

In this case, the battle for the theoretical center was not waged by the French founders of these discourses against the cultural scholars in postcolonial societies. Rather this battle was waged primarily by postcolonial scholars in major Western universities, who sought to grasp and transcend the errors and failings of the "original" postcolonial theorists through the categories and deconstructive strategies of post-structuralism. Among this group of largely diasporic scholars are V.Y. Mudimbe, Gyatri Spivak, Homi Bhabha, Stuart Hall, Sylvia Wynter, Edouard Glissant, Adlai Murdoch, David Scott, Antonio Benetez-Rojo, Michaeline Crichlow, and Achille Mbembe. In the Caribbean, a major exception to this trend has been the literary and calypso critic Gordon Rohlehr. Centering himself in the sounds, words, and movements of nation dance, Rohlehr has sought to develop the tradition of criticism Kamau Brathwaite has called nation language (1990:20; 2004:23–49).

Over the past three decades, the above group of scholars has undertaken careful post-structuralist readings and critiques of the "original" postcolonial texts with the hope of diagnosing the crises that had overtaken their projections. This rise of post-structuralist theory was not confined to the arts such as literature and philosophy, but also the social sciences, sociology and anthropology in particular, as works of Julian Go, Arturo Escobar and Michaeline Crichlow make clear

## GYATRI SPIVAK

Perhaps the most authoritative and revealing of these post-structuralist readings of the postcolonial situation is Gyatri Spivak's *A Critique of Postcolonial Reason*. In this work, the author's primary aim is the opening up of a distinct Spivakian discursive space in which it will be possible to read and deconstruct the "original" postcolonial texts, along with the political and epistemic practices they have produced. In other words, in spite of rooting the very concept of critique in Kant, Hegel and Marx, Spivak's critique of postcolonial reason is going to be a Derridean one. Here the aim of the deconstructive critique is not directly the categories and binaries of Western reason but those of postcolonial reason. These need to be examined in the mirror of differance, "the open-ended deconstructive noting of writing as the structure that assures the possibility of meaning in the absence of the sender" (38). This is the center of differance that will displace God, Spirit, the mode of production, the plantation, or institutional dependency as centers or senders. Differance is a center that is not a center, a sender that is not a sender.

Within this de-centered Spivakian semio-linguistic framework a number of crucial concepts move in binary oppositional dances that are different from their movements in the "original" postcolonial texts and the practices associated with them. These include male/female, colonizer/colonized, colonialism/neocolonialism, Spirit/history, Derridean/non-Derridean. Most important for Spivak is the binary of the native informant/master. She links the native informant directly with the subaltern woman who is foreclosed, in the Lacanian sense, in the discourse of the master and thus is unable to speak. Further, the native informant has an "imagined and impossible perspective," which is not strong enough to succeed with a mere reversal of masters like Kant, Hegel, or Marx. Thus, standing firmly on the deconstructive ground of Prospero's reason, Spivak suggests that the native informant can no longer "continue to act out the part of Caliban" (37). Such an oppositional strategy is no longer viable in the globalized capitalism of the post-Soviet era. But the native informant's impossible perspective is one that permits Spivak to supply her with Derridean powers. It is the distinct oppositional play of these binary oppositions that gives this Spivakian discursive space its originality and singular textuality. It is from this perspective that Spivak will read the Brahmanic tradition, the *Bhagavad Gita*, Aurobindo, Radhakrishnan and others.

As the various texts of the "original" postcolonial writer enter this Spivakian discursive space, the primary goal is to displace their surface features, whether these are political, religious, nationalist or creolist, and to expose their deeper levels of uncontrolled semiotic play and possibly the key level of arche-writing. What Spivak finds at these deeper levels are not the anti-colonial strategies of reversing binary oppositions but hidden subterranean practices of complicity between strategies of local hegemony and the axiomatics of imperialism. In short, the primary yield of Spivak's deconstructive critique is that in spite of the conscious attempts in the original texts to reverse the ordering of many of the key binaries on which European imperialism established its hegemony, the deeper *a priori* and semio-linguistic reality is one of complicity born of the categorical entrapment of the identity and discourses of the colonized in those of the colonizer. Thus, Spivak reads Sri Aurobindo, Sarvepalli Radhakrishnan and other anti-colonial nationalists as displacements of what she "metonymically named 'Hegel'" (1992:62). This is the condition that explains our neocolonial predicament and why we have not been able to get out of it.

## MICHAELINE CRICHLOW

Another systematic and careful application of post-structuralist theory to the texts of earlier postcolonial writers is the work of Michaeline Crichlow in *Globalization and the Postcolonial Imagination*. The primary deconstructive aim of this text is the de-centering of the plantation as the source or "resting place" of the hybrid processes of cultural mixing of Caribbean creole theory. Having removed Caribbean creole theory from its resting place somewhere in the plantation, Crichlow's second aim is to re-inscribe the mixing activities of this theory in the codes of the "eBay imagination" produced by globalization and out-migration from the Caribbean. In this expanded context, the semiotic movements that result in creolization would no longer refer specifically to Caribbean processes of cultural mixing, but to the cultural politics of the eBay-like space that Caribbean people enter as they migrate to various parts of our increasingly globalized world. This new cultural politics would be a non-essentialist practice of ongoing and open-ended processes of diasporic place-making in an expanded eBay-like world.

Crichlow executes this re-orienting of Caribbean creole theory by remodeling the activities of Caribbean diasporic subjects on the Derridean description of arche-writing and differance. In other words, it was through a re-conceptualization of the place-making agency of the Caribbean diasporic subject as differance that Crichlow was able to perform this reconceptualization and inaugurate what she calls "the post-creole imagination."

Within this differance-empowered eBay world, Crichlow has a distinct set of binary oppositions operating. These include postcolonial nation/diaspora, cultural mixing/place-making, plantation/eBay world, essentialist/anti-essentialist, and Derridean/non-Derridean. As in the case of Spivak, it is the semiotic play between these oppositions that constitutes the body of the text. Also contributing to the composition this textual body is Crichlow's ethno-historical work in peasant communities in St. Lucia and Jamaica. This ethno-historical work enables Crichlow to further distinguish her position from that of the members of the Caribbean plantation school, which included economists such as George Beckford and Clive Thomas. These Crichlow now sees as essentialist and outside of the new de-centered and anti-essentialist framework of a differance-orchestrated theory of diasporic place-making. In contrast to Spivak, the colonized or the native informant is not as radically foreclosed and is thus able to speak and to theorize beyond reversing binary oppositions. However, they will not be able to defeat the deconstructive masters in this discursive exchange. Like Aurobindo and Radhakrishnan in the case of Spivak, they remain trapped in old and centered orderings of binary oppositions that inhibit their entry into the new globalized eBay world of our current conjuncture.

## DAVID SCOTT

Our third major attempt to apply post-structuralist theory to the late 1970s crisis of the postcolonial societies is David Scott's *Conscripts of Modernity*. Like Spivak and Crichlow, Scott makes a clear distinction between the theories of the postcolonial nationalists and the post-structuralist theories of postcolonial studies. From Scott's perspective the former are all essentialists, believers in fixed identities, universals, absolute centers and historical necessities. In short, they are all trapped in the *a priori* categories of the Western Enlightenment and hence are "conscripts of modernity." It is to this situation of categorical conscription that Scott attributes the failures of our postcolonial projects of nation building.

To get past this crisis, Scott suggests that the field of postcolonial studies must reject the revolutionary categories with which postcolonial nationalists had attempted to grasp their past, present and future. These temporal categories must be uprooted and re-inscribed within those of the writerly or Derridean text. In particular, essentialist and romantic notions of a revolutionary nationalist future must be replaced with an anti-essentialist poetics of postcolonial history. To achieve this reframing of the future, the self-understanding and political practices of the postcolonial nationalists, Scott turns to Hayden White's semio-linguistic theory of the forms of narrative. In particular, Scott is interested in how historical relations between past, present and future are semiotically emplotted in different forms of narrative, and are thus the works of subterranean language games rather than the conscious work of a revolutionary nationalist or a rational sociologist. Scott uses Hayden White to suggest that romantic conceptions of self and future are semio-linguistic illusions, the play of a language game created by the emplotting powers of a

romantic mode of self-narration. Scott further argues that James was such a
semotic conscript of this romantic language game and that it was the realization of this entrapment that led to the addition of a note on the tragic to the
1963 edition of *The Black Jacobins*. This tragic reading Scott thinks captures
more accurately our postcolonial present and it is the re-inscription that he
recommends to his colleagues in the field of postcolonial studies.

## THE YIELD OF THESE POST-STRUCTURALIST
## RE-INSCRIPTIONS

In assessing the yield of these turns to post-structuralism, it is important to
note that not all postcolonial scholars who made this turn have deployed
post-structuralism in the hegemonic fashion of the three cases examined
above. For many, it has been used primarily as a strategy of textual interpretation, which has enhanced or left intact the anti-colonial voices or the original and later postcolonial writers. In others, it has functioned largely as part
of a more egalitarian theoretical dialogue between North and South. This
more egalitarian deployment can be seen in the work of Caribbean scholars
such as Edouard Glissant, Sylvia Wynter and Adlai Murdoch. Wynter's is
definitely not a voice that has been foreclosed or one that has been con-
scripted, and neither is Murdoch's. Rather, Wynter takes for granted her
ability to theorize our increasingly globalized condition from the perspective
of the challenges confronting the postcolonial countries.

In the case of Murdoch, the egalitarian balance struck between Caribbean
creole theory and post-structuralism is right on point. He begins with the
clear acknowledgment that it is the unstable creolizing and migrant factors in
the formation of Caribbean identities that makes them of interest to the
"nonoriginary nature of identity in its postmodern, poststructuralist guise"
(578). This convergence of interest from different prior locations becomes
the basis for an egalitarian and highly nuanced exchange between Caribbean
creole theory and post-structuralism in which the former retains its voice and
its hold on the center. Thus it becomes a model for the kind of thinking and
writing we should be doing in this period that has followed the decline of
post-structuralism.

However, before turning to such models, our more immediate concern
here will be with the hegemonic strategies of replacing, from their founding
centers up to their surface claims, the discourses of the postcolonial nationalists with a post-structuralist infrastructure.

Among the more notable inconsistencies in this hegemonic deploying of
post-structuralist theory is its failure to subject this theory to the standards
and principles of critique applied to the original postcolonial writers. First,
there was no rigorous interrogating of whether or not Derrida really suc-

ceeded in his attempt to overthrow metaphysics and its related essentializing practices. The ambiguity inherent in difference as a center that is not a center is uncritically accepted and deployed as a stronger and more foundational center against other centers. This problem of founding centers has been and still is at the heart of metaphysical traditions in both North and South. Thus the founding claims of post-structuralism should have been the occasion for an egalitarian and wide-ranging discussion about the metaphysical centers that have grounded the thought of the original postcolonial writers and the non-center of post-structuralism.

However, this is precisely what did not happen in these cases of hegemonic deployment. Instead, there was the unjustified assumption that the project of overthrowing metaphysics was a successful undertaking. But past experiences have shown that metaphysical arguments have never really been final or complete. Derrida was very aware of this difficulty (1978:281). Thus if indeed Derrida was not successful in his overthrowing of metaphysics (as I think), then his case for the founding status of difference becomes one of the most sophisticated metaphysical arguments against metaphysics. Evidence of this failure can be seen in the strong tendency to center signs that reflect the play of difference in ways that are not consistent with a successful critique and overthrow of metaphysics. In other words, the establishing of the priority of difference over centers such as God, the self, or the mode of production have only been completed with the aid of standard metaphysical strategies for establishing the priority of one center or one dimension of reality over another.

The case that the Derridean revolt against metaphysics may not have been successful is further suggested by the fact that like other metaphysical positions it has its own grand narrative, in spite of its rejection of such narratives. If the liberation of the proletariat or of a colonized people are grand narratives, then the following question must arise: Is the liberation of the writerly sign from its subordination to speech another such grand narrative that is internal to the deep structure of post-structuralism? This is a question that scholars like Crichlow, Spivak and Scott would have asked had they applied the same standards and principles of critique to post-structuralism.

Also very striking in all three cases of hegemonic deployment is the ahistorical approach taken to the deploying of post-structuralism. Thus we get no interrogating of whether or not the particular shift in the binary relations between speech and writing was a response to specific development in French or Western society. Such possibilities of historicizing the rupture that led to the emergence of difference to greater visibility and thus of reading it in the light of the centers and categories of other discourses are not explored in these three cases. Indeed such possibilities are prohibited by the arche-center status given to signs that reflect the play of difference on the assumption of a successful overthrow of metaphysics.

Similarly foreclosed by the arche-status of these signs is the possibility that the writerly revolution was a displacement, onto the semiotic level, of the insurrectionary movements in France and the wider West that we marked by 1968. Spivak in particular should have raised this possibility of displacement as she raised it more than once in her critique of the postcolonial nationalists. In sum, these familiar marks of blocked possibilities of displacement, ahistorical abstraction, grand narratives, a center that is not a center, meta-linguistic arguments justifying the priority of differance over other possible centers all point to the metaphysical nature of Derrida's arguments, and thus to the possibility that his revolt against earlier forms of metaphysics and their binary hierarchies may not have been as successful as assumed by Spivak, Crichlow, and Scott.

If this assumption of the victory over metaphysics turns out to be incorrect, then the hegemonic imposition of the categories of post-structuralism become another case of a metaphysically imposed form of determinism, this time a semio-linguistic one. As in other cases pointed out by post-structualists, such forms of determinism are authoritarian epistemic strategies. Thus without greater certainty of the successful overthrow of metaphysics, the imposition of the founding categories of post-structuralism on the discourses of the original and later postcolonial writers become a truly problematic form of hegemonic capture. The inequality that becomes necessary at the communicative level in all three cases is thus a reflection of the already assumed semiotic supremacy of a center of signs orchestrated by the play of differance. This is a hierarchical relation without which the discourses of Crichlow, Spivak and Scott could not have been so readily imposed on the texts of the original postcolonial writers. The foreclosure, conscription or silencing of these writers are as much a requirement of this mode of deploying post-structuralism as they were of earlier imperial discourses.

This wide gap between the actual speaking of the colonized and their restricted voices within these cases of the hegemonic deploying of post-structuralism is clearest in the exchange between Aurobindo and Derrida in Spivakian space. Within the categories of this space, Aurobindo is restricted to speaking primarily as a postcolonial nationalist. As such Aurobindo's reading of the *Bhagavad Gita* becomes "a de-racialized" version of "the entire Hegelian graph of spirit's journey" (1999:63). This is truly a most troubling statement. It makes very clear the form of hegemonic capture that is basic to Spivak's discursive space and the epistemic shackles that it imposes on postcolonial knowledge production. Aurobindo is so much more than a nationalist, and is certainly not a foreclosed voice or a conscript who can only displace the tensions of the older opposition, colonialism/nationalism, onto more contemporary North/South relations.

If ever there was an occasion for an egalitarian exchange of ideas it is between Aurobindo and Derrida or between Aurobindo and Hegel. In addition to his nationalist writings, Aurobindo's highly original theories of spirituality match and go beyond those of Hegel. The only way to be fair to both is to put them in a more open and egalitarian conversation. Further, in *The Secret of the Vedas* and *The Future of Poetry*, Aurobindo develops a theory of language that should have been put in an egalitarian conversation with Derrida's as it is vital for his reading of the *Gita*. Using the case of Sanskrit, Aurobindo suggests that the origins of language are to be found in key mantric vibrations or seed-sounds that contained the potential for all future linguistic development. These originary vibrations were connected to a plurality of mantras, ideas and significations. These mantras, ideas and significations represented the outer or material forms of language. At the same time, these originary vibrations or seed-sounds were also capable of echoing even more foundational vibrations on what Aurobindo called the supramental level of consciousness—a level that opens them to knowledge of Divinity.

Having established these inner and outer dimensions of language, Aurobindo then turned to an examination of basic patterns in the historical evolution of languages, such as Tamil, Greek and Latin, out of the hypothesized supramentally connected seed-sounds. From this historical/evolutionary analysis, Aurobindo suggests that a dominant tendency in the development of languages has been toward more fixed and standardized forms of representation and away from the more fluid forms of outer representations associated with the more originary and supramentally orchestrated mantric sounds. This movement toward more fixed forms of representation Aurobindo referred to as fossilization. In turn, this fossilization of linguistic representation has had the effect of cutting us off from the originary sounds contained in the Vedic mantras—and thus from the supramental vibrations that give us knowledge of Divinity.

In Aurobindo's world, anything that actively cuts us off from the supramental plane, such as the guna-based self-formative activities of the ego, must be subject to "silencing" or suspension by some type of yogic or meditative practice. Similarly, Aurobindo argues that the fixing or fossilizing activities of the material or outer dimensions of language must be silenced and transcended, on a model comparable to the silencing of the guna-based activities of the ego, if it is not to be an increasing barrier to the supramental plane.

This need to practice the silencing of language in Aurobindo is clearly comparable to Derrida's call for the deconstruction of fixed hierarchies of linguistic binaries. This comparability in their philosophies of language should have been the occasion for an egalitarian exchange including their positions on the founding centers of language. What are we to make of the structural similarities between Aurobindo's notion of originary vibrations containing the full potential of language and Derrida's arche-writing? What are we to make of the structural differences between Derrida's arche-writing that is without a sender, and Aurobindo's mantric sounds with a supramental sender? Particularly in the context of a postcolonial exchange such as this, we should not just assume that Derrida's center of arche-writing can imperially displace and replace Aurobindo's mantric sounds. A much more egalitarian exchange between these founding centers of language is called for here. In this exchange, a good question would have been: How useful would it be to consider Derridean deconstruction as a yoga for suspending or breaking through the *maya* of language? A bad and clearly reductionist suggestion would have been that Derridean deconstruction is a Westernized version of the Aurobindan graph of the noise made by the representational practices of language and their silencing.

In sum, what emerges from these cases is a reinforcing of an older imperially induced invisibility of Caliban's reason. This faculty is under-represented, its nature systematically distorted, and its revolutionary or transformative capabilities severely restricted. Caliban's reason as a distinct knowledge-producing faculty is never really described and analyzed as an epistemic formation in its own right. Too often it is treated as a variant of Western reason and thus in need of the medicine of post-structuralist deconstruction. In *Caliban's Reason*, I tried to outline some of the distinctive features of the concept and practice of reason in the Caribbean, and how they differed from the hegemonic and racist conceptions of reason that developed in the West. I suggested that in the Caribbean, anti-colonial and postcolonial reason can be represented by the image of an intertextually embedded vine rather than that of a tall imperial tree that dominates its surrounding environment. Given these differences, it become necessary to ask if the best medicine for postcolonial reason is indeed the same as that needed by Western reason. Did Caliban's reason really need the uprooting of its metaphysical center? And if so, was that re-centering the one produced by the inverting of the founding binary between speech and writing? These are some of the cautions that would have arisen from a more egalitarian exchange between post-structuralist reason and postcolonial reason.

## THE DECLINE OF NEOLIBERALISM AND POST-STRUCTURALISM

As the hegemonic rise of the discourses of neoliberalism and post-structuralism was the result of impositions, their decline has been inseparable from the loss of power and cultural capital that made their imposition possible. In the case of neoliberalism, it was the financial collapse of 2008 (the Great Recession) that was the disabling event. This crash not only severely damaged the credibility of neoliberal theory but also disabled the post-1980 U.S. model of financial accumulation, which was based on profiting from the accumulating of massive trade deficits with the rest of the world—particularly Germany, Japan and China. The U.S. had been able to do this for two basic reasons. First, with the 1971 collapse of the gold-backed U.S. dollar standard for trading, it was largely replaced by un-backed U.S. dollars. As the major reserve currency, the U.S. was essentially free to cover its trade deficits with dollars that it printed. Second, to turn this special advantage into a major model of accumulation, countries having trade surpluses with the U.S. were for financial reasons constrained to reinvest most of these dollars in U.S. stocks, bonds, debt, or to invest directly in the U.S. In this way, these growing trade deficits were balanced by a surplus on the capital account, which produced dramatic expansions in the American financial sector. However, after the crash of 2008, this model of financial accumulation no longer worked so well. This in turn reduced the capacity and appeal of neoliberal models of postcolonial development that were based on exporting to the U.S.

With regard to the decline of post-structuralism, its loss of hegemony is inseparable from the passing of its two major architects: Foucault and Derrida. As we have already suggested, there were many unresolved problems in post-structuralist theory that their disciples failed to take up and carry forward. Hence the gradual decline in the influence of this theory.

This near simultaneous decline in the hegemonic power of post-structuralism and neoliberalism has created a new epistemic situation for postcolonial studies. For some postcolonial scholars, particularly those still wedded to these two discourses, this new situation may be a crisis of some severity. However, for others it has been a major opportunity for new thinking. I have been suggesting that the decline of these two discourses has created an opening for postcolonial scholars to retake control of the direction of both economic and critical thinking in the Global South (2017). Further, to embark on such a path of re-capture, postcolonial theorists will have to return to the peak periods of local economic and critical theorizing before the surrendering of control. The purpose of returning to those moments would be to carefully assess what was true and false in what we were saying at the time.

## TO THE RE-STARTING POINT

To make the return to those crucial moments of postcolonial theorizing called for by the current opening, I think it best to begin with the views and responses of some of the "postcolonial nationalists" to the onset and deepening of the neocolonial crisis of our postcolonial era. Focusing once again on the Caribbean region, I will begin with Lloyd Best. In his essay honoring fellow economist George Beckford, "Independence and Responsibility: Self-knowledge as an Imperative," Best is angry and very disappointed with "the mess" that we have made of Caribbean postcolonial economies. He identifies

three basic regional visions that have guided Caribbean economic development between 1962 and the early 1980s. These were the plantation economics of the New World Group, of which he was a founding member; a Marxist
school of economics, which he associated with Clive Thomas; and a more
Arthur Lewis–oriented approach, which he associated with Courtney Black-
man. Best attributes most of the responsibility for the "complete shambles"
in our economies, after almost three decades of political independence, to the
first two visions. He insists that we are responsible and cannot use excuses
such as negative trends in the global economy or corporate imperialism.

However, the primary reason that Best suggested for why our economic
theories were so wrong is the fact that we were not at the center of our own
theorizing. He pointed repeatedly to this wide gap between the production of
knowledge about our economies and knowledge of ourselves as active subjects in these economies. How did we get ourselves into this paradoxical
situation? Best's answer was that in importing Western Keynesian and Marx-
ian economic discourses we substituted the subjects of these discourses for
ourselves. In suggesting a solution to this condition of epistemic entrapment,
Best emphasized the paying of greater attention to the specificity of place in
the construction of theories. By increasing this awareness of the specificity of
our place, the Caribbean, we just might be able to get ourselves back to the
center of our economic theories and hopefully rescue our economies.

Kari Polanyi Levitt, Best's longtime collaborator is equally strong in her
response to the neocolonial crisis of Caribbean postcolonial economies. She
has chronicled with great care the declines in some of our major economies
such as Jamaica and Guyana. However, Levitt is not convinced that the
theories produced in this insurgent period are as far off the mark as Best. She
continues to track important changes in the global economy and to point out
that she and Best never produced the fourth model that they promised, which
would have completed the plantation theory of Caribbean economies.

In his many responses to what he has called our period of "permanent
crisis," Clive Thomas also addressed the distortions and misrepresentation
that have come with the importing of economic theories from the West.
However, in contrast to Best, Thomas insists that the greatest responsibility
for this state of permanent crisis lies with the distortions and misrepresentation that have come from the application of mainstream Western economics
to the growth and development problems of our Caribbean region. For example, like Levitt, Thomas takes strong issue with the liberal/neoliberal view of
the world economy as a benign and enabling environment for developing
economies. Rather, he has stayed with the older dependency view of the
world economy developed by Raul Prebisch and others. Thomas also objects
strongly to the claim of liberal/neoliberal theory that social development is
an exogenous or "A" factor in the process of economic growth. In spite of the
onset of the crisis, he continued to hold the view that social development is

an endogenous factor in economic growth and development. Thus in the hegemonic rise of neoliberalism Thomas perceived a threat that would "stifle the impulse to creativity and originality in Caribbean thought" (239).

From this brief sampling of the responses of some of the Caribbean "post-colonial nationalists" to the onset of our period of permanent crisis, it should be clear that there was a definite awareness that along with the technical difficulties of theorizing and growing Caribbean economies, there was the more basic problem of the absence or the misrepresenting of ourselves in the technical economic knowledge we were producing. Thus if we are to take full advantage of the epistemic possibilities of the current opening, this paradoxical issue must be clearly addressed.

## GETTING OURSELVES BACK TO THE CENTER

To return ourselves to the center of our discourses and close existing gaps between the production of technical knowledge and self-knowledge, it is clear that we will have to build on Best's suggestion about rooting ourselves more firmly in the specifics of the Caribbean as a distinct place. In making this suggestion, Best had two things in mind: first, a deeper linking of our creative imagination to the flora, fauna, mountains, seas and stars of our region through metaphors, analogies, allegories and other symbolic devices. The second thing that Best had in mind was engaging what he called "the Divinity" within through a similar set of symbolic devices. When these symbolically mediated connections with nature and Divinity in a particular place are strong, secret dialogues open of great cultural significance. This responsiveness of nature and Divinity to the human psyche is what Best calls the Muse or Oracle of a place. Being able to engage the Caribbean Muse is vital for returning ourselves to the center of our discourses.

Sylvia Wynter's suggestion for how we can re-establish ourselves at the center of our discourses is also very useful here. Concerned about the systematic misrepresentation of people of African descent in Western literature, Wynter made extensive use of post-structuralism to diagnose and resist this marginalizing and distorting of Black subjectivity in Western literature. For Wynter, we are not only trapped in the Western episteme but in its liminal categories (1984:22–25). As the polar opposites of the founding or central categories of epistemes, liminal categories are the ones that systematically under-represent, distort and devalue their contents. Thus to use and internalize discourses in which we fall into liminal categories is a sure way to remove ourselves from the center of our discourses. For Wynter, the only way in which we can return to the center of our discourses and adequately represent our place is by delinking or breaking out of the Western episteme and creating one of our own—a "postcolonial episteme." Like Best's calls for new treaties of sensibility and greater attention to specifics of place, the project of creating a postcolonial episteme within our existing neocolonial framework has proved to be an extremely difficult undertaking. Epistemic breaks have been made only to be followed by another hegemonic capture, and a relinking to the West on more dependent and unequal terms. Thus we need to look at what additional factors, such as institutional ones, must be taken into account if we are to break this cycle of hegemonic capture and displacement from the center of our discourses.

## RE-LINKING THE EPISTEMIC AND THE INSTITUTIONAL

One of the consequences of the hegemonic rise of neoliberalism and post-structuralism has been a displacing of institutions from the center of social analysis. In the case of post-structuralism, this displacement was effected through the centering of writing and its related discourse-constitutive powers. In the case of neoliberalism, the displacement of institutions was effected through the centering of the market and its discourse-constitutive powers. As we have seen, externally dependent institutions have been a major center anchoring several strains of Latin American, African and Caribbean postcolonial discourses. Thus as part of the rethinking of the epistemic and the institutional levels of analysis, we will have to take up quite explicitly the practices by which we have established our discursive centers and the place of the institutional as a competing candidate for the center. Having looked at this issue of Caribbean discursive centers, we will then link this epistemic analysis to the institutional contexts in which such epistemic decisions and choices have been made. In doing so, it is my hope to be contributing to new and more successful delinkings from the Western episteme.

The current opening gives us an opportunity to rethink the problem of centers in general, the displacing of institutions, and the possibilities of performing differently in the years ahead. To re-establish ourselves at the center of our discourses, we are going to have to be more confident that we can occupy and hold this strategic position in spite of the attempts that others will make to displace us. To increase our confidence in being at the center of our discourses, we will definitely have to better appreciate and make more visible our history of establishing discursive centers, and in this way increase its cultural capital. The establishing of discursive centers is at its core a metaphysical undertaking. Thus to make more visible our history of establishing discursive centers, we will have to make more explicit our metaphysical tradition, the centers it has established and the strategies it has employed in these undertakings. However, if there is an area of our thinking that has not separated itself from the West, and continues to depend on the West, it is that of metaphysics. This is the rupture that should now concern us; the new metaphysical turn in our postcolonial intellectual life that we must make. The ease with which Scott and Crichlow can ignore the deep roots of post-structuralism in a very French/German metaphysical tradition, with distinct concepts of reason and practices of center formation, is a good indicator of how weakly rooted we are in our own metaphysical tradition, its concepts of reason and history of center formation. This pattern of over-identification/under-identification must change if we are going to re-establish ourselves at the center of our discourses.

In the case of the Afro-Caribbean population, the metaphysical foundations of the African and Afro-Christian periods consisted of the set of arguments by which Spirit was established as the center around which all other beings and things were constellated. In the case of the Indo-Caribbean population, the metaphysical foundations of the Indian and Indo-Christian periods consisted of a different set of arguments by which Spirit as Brahman was also established as the center around which everything else was constellated. However, in the secular historicist/poeticist period that followed the Afro- and Indo-Christian periods, there were important shifts in the metaphysical foundations of our thinking. Spirit ceased to be the obvious center and found itself competing with other factors such as matter, self, art, reason, history, race, class, gender, discipline, states, or markets, for this originary locus. Our metaphysics thus became the set of arguments by which the priority of the claim to the center of one of these factors was justified over those of others.

Emerging more clearly in this period of more fluid centers was the vine of Caribbean reason with its two major branches: historicism and poeticism. Inseparable from history and poetics, Caribbean reason was not logocentric, and as in the case of Best, explicitly engaged its poetic foundations and dimensions. As a result, I have described the metaphysical foundations of this period as an improvisational, jazz-like creative realism. In this metaphysical tradition, whether in the cases of Du Bois, James, Fanon or Wynter, we can recognize many of the above factors competing for the center position. What we don't see is a fixed prioritizing of these discourse-constitutive fundamentals around the concept of reason. Rather, what we do see is the strong tendency to raise the creative act in its spontaneous movements to the center and not any of its specific creations including those of reason. This history of creative realist metaphysics should have been the basis for our exchange with post-structuralism.

Given this improvisational foundation and the vine-like nature of Caribbean philosophy, the rise of Derridean deconstruction should have been a great occasion for an egalitarian conversation close to what we find in Wynter and Murdoch, rather than a direct taking over of the center. Thus in this period of the opening one of the first things that we must undertake is the reviving of this distinct Caribbean creative realist metaphysical tradition, re-activate its center-establishing powers, and through its discursive agency contribute to the process of re-placing ourselves at the center of our economic and critical discourses.

At the same time that we are working to restore the center-making powers of our metaphysical tradition, we must also be looking anew at the institutional context in which this metaphysical work is being done. In order to bring this institutional context into a clearer focus, we must take greater notice of the peripheral nature of our cultural system as a whole, and in particular its knowledge-producing sector. This sociological dimension of knowledge production has fallen into the liminal category, and thus systemically eclipsed by the discursively centered notions of structure in post-structuralism. The knowledge-producing sector of our cultural system would include our institutions of primary, secondary and tertiary education along with our research centers. The organization of this sector—its internal, external and international relations—shapes the concrete contexts in which specific disciplinary practices of knowledge production will take place, such as producing creole theories or defending dependency theories.

The peripheral nature of postcolonial cultural systems can be seen in the sets of local/imperial dynamics that Rex Nettleford has termed "battles for space" (1993:80). These battles for discursive and institutional space are hegemonic struggles that continue to occur in many disciplinary areas. These hegemonic battles are the structural foundations for distinct patterns of accumulating or dis-accumulating cultural and epistemic capital in the forms of recognition, legitimacy, truth possession, authority or the right to occupy the center. These accumulative/dis-accumulative dynamics help us to understand the oft-repeated rise in power, credibility, status, and hegemony of Western discourses over Caribbean ones, European languages over Afro-Caribbean ones, European music over Indo-Caribbean music, neo-liberal economics over Indo- and Afro-Caribbean economics. The persistence of these zero-sum patterns of epistemic accumulation is systematically linked to our continuing dependence on Western universities, graduate programs, journals, and research centers for the training of too many of the professionals who staff the higher levels of our knowledge-producing sectors. Consequently, addressing these areas of continuing external epistemic dependence must be an integral part of the project of returning ourselves to the center of our discourses.

Also vital to this re-centering project must be a very deliberate returning to the specific battles for space which we lost to neoliberalism and post-structuralism, in order to revaluate the validity of the arguments that we were making at that time. In the case of neoliberalism, we have seen that the particular battle for space was with the structurally oriented economic theories of the dependency school. This insurgent postcolonial discourse peaked with the 1974 adoption by a special session of the UN General Assembly of UNCTAD's call for a New International Economic Order. The systematic attack on the UN by the U.S. after

1980 was a clear indicator of the sharp differences between this call and the neoliberal policies that the West had embarked upon to address their 1970s stagflation and shareholder value crises.

When we return to the scene of this battle after the intervening decades, at least two things stand out. First, among the more notable developments in mainstream Western economics since 2008 has been the rediscovery of the institutional and other non-market factors in the determination of economic behavior and thus the growth of economies. This is clear in the later works of major economists and economic thinkers like Douglass North, Joseph Stiglitz, Jeffrey Sachs, John Gray, and Paul Krugman. As a result, their objections to neoliberalism include their resistance to its excluding of the institutional context from the center, its making of it an exogenous or "A" factor. As we examine their arguments, they echo so many of those made by Prebisch, Beckford, Best, and others, whose ideas contributed to the NIEO proposals. Thus the unequal exchange over markets and institutions between neoliberal and dependency theorists should be an important lesson for us as we retake control over the direction of our economic thinking.

The second point that stands out when we return to the scene of this particular battle for space was the theoretical legitimacy of calling for a re-structuring of the global economy as a vital part of our response to the neo-colonial crisis of our postcolonial economies. In particular, the clearly argued concerns about the need for a different type of mechanism than the IMF for dealing with growing trade deficits, rising instabilities in commodity prices, and in exchange rates after the collapse of the gold/dollar standard have become common fare today. Indeed, they now seem all so reasonable in the light of all the state-led polices (TARP, quantitative easing, zero interest rates) that have been implemented by Western governments to stabilize their banking systems and to contain the fallout from the collapse of 2008. Whether it is the former British prime minister Gordon Brown's recommendations or those of Stiglitz or Sachs, they all include combinations of national and global reforms as appropriate responses for achieving redress. Comparing the actual responses taken to this crisis in the West with those proposed by the NIEO, we have very good reasons for relocating ourselves at the center of our economic discourses.

Finally, in this deliberate returning to the scenes of the hegemonic battles for space, we come to the site of capture by post-structuralism. Earlier we saw that, under the leadership of some of its major postcolonial lieutenants, post-structuralism undertook the de-centering and re-inscribing within its own categories of major Caribbean discourses such as creole theory, plantation theory, Caribbean Marxism, Pan Africanism, and Caribbean nationalism. Particularly in the cases of scholars like Spivak, Scott and Crichlow, we have seen that the center was surrendered without a careful exchange between Caribbean and Indian metaphysical arguments for establishing discursive centers and those that Derrida was making for differance as a center that was not a traditional center. However, with the incompleteness and decline of this project, we are once more on our own. In this period of the opening, Wynter, Harris, Glissant and Murdoch, among others, are good examples of how we should proceed, of what we should take from this encounter with post-structuralism.

In addition to her notion of a postcolonial episteme, Wynter's powerful concept of the mode of producing the human is a classic case of how post-structuralist theory can be used to engage and expand the reach of Caribbean discourses like Black Marxism, creole theory or Pan Africanism. In sharp contrast to Scott's treatment of James's or Crichlow's treatment of creole theory, Wynter's extensive use of post-structuralism does not de-center these theories but gives them a new epistemic grounding and a whole new dimension. It is definitely the kind of thinking that we must undertake now and in the years ahead.

Similarly, in the case of Murdoch, we have another powerful example of how to bring Caribbean creole theory into an egalitarian discourse with the highly valuable aspects of post-structuralist theory. In the patterns of in- and out-migration of Caribbean societies, Murdoch sees the doubleness, the creolizations, the cut and mix, the assimilations and syncretisms that make the region a place of unstable identities. This condition is indeed a major motivation for applying or engaging post-structuralist theory. But are these movements the same as the movements of differance? It is Murdoch's thoughtful hesitation at this crucial juncture that is so important for us now. Recognizing the concrete differences between the movements of creolization and those of differance, Murdoch suggests that rather than "reading the Caribbean subject through current models of postmodernity . . . it might be more fruitful to seek sites of Caribbean identity within longstanding regional patterns of erasure and (re)invention" (578). By doing this, he has been able to increase the subtlety of Caribbean creole discourse without giving an inch in its hold on the center. Without a single stroke of explicit defense the jazz-like metaphysical foundation of Caribbean creole discourse is flawlessly enacted by Murdoch. Clearly on display at its center are the spontaneous moves of creative positing rather than any of its specific but ever-moving creations. They remain consistently in creative and interpretative play with post-structuralsim but are never subsumed or decentered by the latter. Like Wynter, Murdoch becomes a crucial guide as we attempt to re-center ourselves in this period of the opening.

## CONCLUSION

Although our primary focus has been the Caribbean, I believe that a strong case can be made for the operating of similar dynamics in other postcolonial societies. Thus a broader South-to-South dialogue regarding the challenges of the opening would be vital at this time. In particular, the clearer specifying of various metaphysical traditions and putting in the intellectual work needed to increase their epistemic and cultural capital.

## BIBLIOGRAPHY

Aurobindo, Sri. 1971. *The Secret of the Veda*. Pondicherry: Sri Aurobindo Ashram.

Best, Lloyd. 1996. "Independence and Responsibility: Self-knowledge as an Imperative" in Kari Levitt & Michael Witter (eds.), *The Critical Tradition of Caribbean Political Economy*. Kingston: Ian Randle Publishers.

Bhabha, Homi. 1994. *The Location of Culture*. New York: Routledge.

Benetez-Rojo, Antonio. 1996. *The Repeating Island*. Durham: Duke University Press.

Brown, Gordon. 2010. *Beyond the Crash*. London: Free Press.

Crichlow, Michaeline. 2009. *Globalization and the Post-creole Imagination*. Durham: Duke University Press.

Derrida, Jacques. 1978. *Writing and Difference*. Chicago: University of Chicago Press.

Escobar Arturo. 1995. *Development as Discourse*. Princeton: Princeton University Press.

Glissant, Edouard. 1989. *Caribbean Discourse*. Charlottesville: University of Virginia Press.

Go, Julian. 2016. *Postcolonial Thought and Social Theory*. New York: Oxford University Press.

Henry, Paget. 2000. *Caliban's Reason*. New York: Routledge.

———. 2017. "Into the Opening: Caribbean Philosophy After Neoliberalism and Post-structuralism," *Antigua and Barbuda Review of Books*, Vol. 10, No. 1.

Krugman, Paul. 2005. *The Great Unraveling*. New York: W.W. Norton.

Levitt, Kari. 1996. "From Decolonization to Neoliberalism: What We Have Learned About Development" in Kari Levitt & Michael Witter (eds.), *The Critical Tradition of Caribbean Political Economy*. Kingston: Ian Randle Publishers.

Mbembe, Achille. 2017. *Critique of Black Reason*. Durham: Duke University Press.

Mill, J. S. 2018. *Principles of Political Economy*, Vol. 1. London: Routledge

Mudimbe, Valentin. 1988 *The Invention of Africa*. Bloomington: Indiana University Press.

Murdoch, Adlai. 2007. "All Skin Teeth Is Not Grin," *Callaloo*, Vol. 30, No. 2.

Nettleford, Rex. 1993. *Inward Stretch, Outward Reach*. London: Macmillan.

North, Douglass. 2007. *Institutions Institutional Change and Economic Performance*. New York: Cambridge University Press.

Rohlehr, Gordon. 2004. *A Scuffling of Islands*. Port of Spain: Lexicon Trinidad.

———. 1990. *Calypso and Society in Pre-independence Trinidad*. Port of Spain: Gordon Rohlehr.

Sachs, Jeffrey. 2017. *Building the New American Economy*. New York: Columbia University Press.

Scott, David. 2004. *Conscripts of Modernity*. Durham: Duke University.

Spivak, Gayatri. 1999. *A Critique of Postcolonial Reason*. Cambridge: Harvard University Press.

Stiglitz, Joseph. 2016. *Rewriting the Rules of the American Economy*. New York: W.W. Norton.

Thomas, Clive. 1996. "The Crisis of Development, Theory and Practice: A Caribbean Perspective" in K. Levitt & M. Witter (eds.), *The Critical Tradition of Caribbean Political Economy*. Kingston: Ian Randle Publishers.

Wynter, Sylvia. 1984. "The Ceremony Must Be Found," *Boundary 2*, No. 12.

## Chapter Three

# Between "Post-Colonial" and "Postcolonial"

*Mauritian Fiction as a Paradigm for Literary Postcoloniality in "Different Degrees"*

## Markus Arnold

At[1] the crossroads of histories, cultures, languages and religions, home to diasporic and post-diasporic communities with origins from three continents, Mauritius constitutes a particularly fruitful territory to discuss multiple post-colonial identities, in terms of geographical, cultural, social, and ethnic be-longing. Colonized by the Dutch, the French, and the British, subject to migratory movements from Europe, Africa and Asia, and independent since 1968, the island located in the South-Western Indian Ocean offers a rich and diverse literary production: a long tradition in French going back to the eighteenth century, English writing from the 1930s onward, and Creole texts starting with independence, as well as other minor languages, let alone the differences between publications inside and outside the island. Over these last twenty years, one can observe in Mauritian literature a certain aesthetic, thematic, and poetic innovation. Francophone novelists such as Ananda Devi, Carl de Souza, Nathacha Appanah, and Amal Sewtohul have recently gained critical and scholarly attention through their subversive, demystifying, and anti-exoticizing texts as well as their complex ways of interrogating issues of identity. A mere glimpse at these contemporary texts shows various recurrent thematic, stylistic, and narrative features: the construction of racial, gender, and social identities, the quest of history and memory, the imagina-tion of the island space and its place in contemporary globalization, the role of the writer and the positioning of his work in transnational literary configu-rations, just to name a few. Yet these authors are mostly published abroad and their works differ in many respects not only from locally released texts, but also from less-known writings in other languages: English, Creole, Hindi or Chinese. In its linguistic diversity, the Mauritian literary field—as far as one can speak in this specific case about a "field" in the Bourdieusian sense—clearly proves to be unequal and heterogeneous.

In a recent monograph, I have attempted a detailed comparative discussion of this diverse and conflicting literary creation—more specifically from the perspective of contemporary novel writing in French and English—revealing tendencies and dominant characteristics currently found in the island's literary productions, where motifs such as identity, violence, and interculturality are omnipresent, and where one can see numerous attempts to negotiate the writers' position at the postcolonial island "periphery" (Arnold 2017). It provides an inquiry into how the writers approach the complexities of the multicultural nation; in other words, how the question of postcolonial identity—in its plural manifestation—inscribes itself in the Mauritian novel. The present chapter thus constitutes an analytic continuation of this comparative work, as well as other articles. In order to acknowledge major traits in the island's literary expressions without minimizing their diversity and complexity, and to avoid such analytic reductionism which abusively amalgamates very different ideological and esthetic directions under the unique term "postcolonial," I argue here for a more nuanced reading method. It deduces from contemporary novel writing on the island, analyzed in several studies, two *regimes of discursivity and textuality* conceptualized under the terms—both contrastive and complementary—of "post-colonial" and "postcolonial." Establishing and thinking these notions enables to set a critical frame of reference for interpreting Mauritian texts. It is also to be understood more generally as an attempt to nuance, reconsider and make operative postcolonial terminology that has often become vague in critical debate, where every text from the Global South or by a writer from a previously colonized country would automatically become "postcolonial."

Indeed although certain scholars have engaged a displacement from the category of the postcolonial to the global (Spivak 2003), and others even claimed the end of the postcolonial paradigm in favor of new configurations (transnationalism, diaspora, migration, cosmopolitanism, decoloniality, etc.), it is arguably still relevant to critically examine a literary text in the light of colonialism's impact on its (author's) referential cultures; not to mention the fact that the label "postcolonial" does not exclude other complementary categories of analysis. Put differently, albeit the controversies it stirred, the term remains indeed "both a way of reading and a critical method anticipating a future beyond colonialism in all its forms" (Zabus 2015, 1). The general objective of this chapter is then to "dig beneath the surface of labels"[2] in order to take hold of the plural and complex realities of postcolonial literatures. More specifically, it will introduce and discuss this "post-colonial"-"postcolonial" reading method, show its application in certain novels from the island, and argue for Mauritian novel-writing as a paradigm for postcolonial literary production at large, thus implying a possible application of the scheme for other literary fields/spaces. By attempting to find dominant characteristics and structures in this heterogeneity of expressions and forms, the critical method is opposed to the idea of fixed taxonomies. It operates more in the spirit of *unstable and permeable dividing lines*, imagining some sort of *continuum* between two poles on which the texts slide with regard to certain criteria.

This proposition is made well knowing the fact that today, more than ever, authors and texts are strongly defying analytical categories in which critics place and often confine them. One may recall here the debates on "Commonwealth literature" denounced already in the 1980s by Salman Rushdie as a label imposed by the "center" and its *universalizing* tendencies to confer a differential and *particular* identity to "ex-centered" writers. More recently, one can refer to the manifesto of 44 Francophone writers against the presumably neocolonial category "littérature francophone" (Le Bris and Rouaud 2007). Indeed, postcolonial perspectives, maybe more than others, are necessarily located at crossroads of different theoretical approaches. As Bill Ashcroft puts it, postcolonialism is not a master-discourse; on the contrary, it represents both "a creatively undisciplined collection of 'margins'" and a "rhizomic interplay of pursuits" (Ashcroft 2015, 236). In literature, the notion takes into consideration institutional and topological questions, linguistic, esthetic, and poetic elements, as well as social, ideological, and historical contexts. It is then of course reductive to speak about *the* postcolonial as one unitary, homogeneous or coherent theory, school of thought, analytical procedure or positioning of identity. Twenty years ago, scholars such as Ann McClintock or Stephen Slemon warned against epistemological leveling which risks rendering the concept unoperational. Ella Shohat, who sees in post-colonial theory "not only a vibrant space for critical, even resistant scholarship, but also a contested space" because its central term "is susceptible to a blurring of perspectives," proposes for example a more precise articulation as "post-anti-colonial critique" (Shohat 1992, 108, 110). Anglo-Caribbean writer Caryl Phillips had already suggested in 1989 to speak about "post-migratory" or "post-postcolonial" writing (Boehmer 2005, 250).

Obviously, the issue is not (any longer) about temporality with the prefix "post" signifying "after colonialism": all contemporary Mauritian fiction is in this sense *post*-colonial. But since nowadays texts are not homogeneous, since they are informed by a plural heritage, and since they show a panoply of expressions which cannot be judged with the same criteria, this chapter argues in favor of a postcolonial perspective *in different degrees* as far as their specific artistic positions, locations of identity, esthetic tendencies, and discursive engagements are concerned which reflect and fit into the sociopolitical and ethnocultural complexity of today's island space. One might also speak of different *strata*.[3] Indeed, like the multifaceted discipline of postcolonial studies itself, Mauritian literature today is unmistakably influenced by legacies and currents as different as anti-colonial movements, vernacular modes of expression, poststructuralist pattern or postmodern thought. It relates to the local and the global, embraces the particular and the cosmopolitan, is shaped by the ideas of *routes* and *roots*—to refer to the homophones famously theorized by James Clifford (1997)—engages into formal play as well as political commitment. More generally, it unveils shifting solidarities and various reference frames (France, Britain, Africa, India, China) to assert its multiple and processual identities. The typology or grid within which I locate Mauritian literature thus operates in the sense of what Graham Huggan sees as the triple understanding of the postcolonial: a difficult negotiation of the legacies of earlier colonial eras, an equally challenging account of those new forms of colonialism and imperialism that have emerged in today's globalization, but also a setting up of parameters for "imaginative and material transformation" in favor of cultural and political autonomy and more cosmopolitan visions of the world (Huggan 2015, 133). For this purpose of a postcolonial perspective *in different degrees*, several theories—from literary, social and cultural studies—shall now be drawn on.

In one of his essays, Roland Barthes (1964) creates two terms in order to oppose two types of writing: on the one hand, the *écrivant* (or scripter) who, like a clerk, mostly focuses on contents and uses language merely to express what is already there; on the other, the *écrivain* (or writer) who searches in the discursive process in which he's absorbed for new elaborations and meanings. The *écrivain* works on language and style, refuses "simple" testimony and doctrinal thought. He introduces doubt and ambiguity, whereas the *écrivant* uses language as an instrument to convey a message, for example as a matter of urgency, to testify or for critical and political purposes. The question "how to write?" contrasts here with the one "what to write?"; esthetics are opposed to intellect or even ethics. Despite the binary and schematic character of this structuralist typology—Barthes himself had already nuanced his position observing a rising presence of a hybrid *écrivain-écrivant* type—certain aspects in this conceptual opposition seem to be helpful for a critical consideration of the characteristics and functions of contemporary fiction, especially in the postcolonial field. There are indeed writers who tend to teach and inform, who overtly use didactics, campaign for a cause and want to explain the world. Others focus on style and form and their commitment lies predominantly in the text which becomes the mediator of interrogating the world's complexities, of setting up ambivalence and indetermination. The ones bring in clear answers and more than often closure, while the others introduce questions and leave us with uncertainties and the word's troubling polyphony. One could thus think of a contrastive model with a porous dividing line between more pragmatic, monological and ideologically transparent texts on the one hand; ambiguous, dialogical and even paradoxical writings on the other.

In African Francophone studies, Barthes' *écrivant* finds an echo with Bernard Mouralis's notion of "counter literature" (Mouralis 1975) which bears many similarities to Ashcroft, Griffith and Tiffin's "writing back" paradigm (Ashcroft et al. 2005), where the term "postcolonial" was introduced to the literary field by focusing on the texts' ethics of resistance and identity politics. More recently, one can find resonances with Charles Bonn (2003, 2006) who draws on Jean-Marc Moura's notion of the "postcolonial scenography" (Moura 1999)—inspired both by Dominique Maingueneau's formula of the "scenography" (Maingueneau 1993) and postcolonial theory—in order to see the multiple relationships the Francophone postcolonial text establishes with its socio-cultural and historic environment. In the narrower context of Maghrebi literature, Bonn speaks of initial postcolonial models: an "anthropological scenography" and a "scenography of rupture." From the 1980s onwards, these models seem to be increasingly supplemented by postmodern scenographies, which—going beyond traditional postures and their collective, often Manichean and militant stances—seem to correspond more to the *écrivain*-typology.

The notions "*écrivant-écrivain,*" "counter-literature" and the different applications of "postcolonial scenography" are useful starting points in order to read the complexities and heterogeneities of the emerging literary field of Mauritius and decipher its main characteristics and tendencies. Yet, to specify the hypothesis of *different degrees of postcoloniality* in the contemporary novel of the island—its textual identities, its esthetics, representations, and fictional universes—one can argue in favor of a productive interaction with other approaches from social, cultural, and literary theory.

To start with, let us refer to Zygmunt Bauman's reflections on the contrast between modernity and postmodernity summed up as follows: "If the *modern* 'problem of identity' is how to construct an identity and keep it solid and stable, the *postmodern* 'problem of identity' is primarily how to avoid fixation and keep the options open."[4] The ideological foundations, the social conceptions, the politics of representation, and the mentalities which characterize modernity then concern the postcolonial in three ways: firstly, the colonial enterprise is strongly linked to the modernist project; secondly, modernity contrasts postmodernity which declares itself emancipated from it; thirdly, modernity has a more or less direct influence on identity configurations in the post-independent nation. The modernist perspective lives towards a project, abandons the "imperfect" presence in the name of a better future, connotes order, homogeneity, determination, a dream which can become

obsession, injunction and tend—in theory and practice—towards totalitarian-
ism. Modernity's foes are confusion, ambiguity, multiple or ambivalent identification; in other words, all the "matter out of place" (Douglas 2007). And
indeed, the nationalist enterprise and the modern state do not give room to
indecision and in-betweenness. It is within postmodernity or "liquid modernity" that identities can (or have to) affirm themselves as plural, heterogeneous, and in movement. The troubling credo of postmodernity—"Nothing can
be known for sure, and anything which is known can be known in a different
way" (Bauman 1997, 53)—has put an end to the grand narratives and their
pillars of unity, clarity, and order.

One should certainly not homogenize the discourse of modernity—Bhabha reminds us of the fact that it is also characterized by temporal ambivalence, contradictions and irresolutions which are often ignored by postmodern theory.[5] It is, however, significant to notice that Paul Gilroy, referring
precisely to Bauman, sets up his paradigm of the "Black Atlantic" as a
"counter-culture of modernity" (Gilroy 1993, 1–40). Bauman's opposition,
articulated around the general antipodes of fixing and unfixing identities, can
thus be operational in the suggested analytical model through/for the Mauritian text. Indeed, modernist logics and economy have not seldom been reiterated in postcolonial nation-building: its claims of identity, uniformity, and
differential modalities are incompatible with floating signifiers and multiple
or ambivalent identification. Frantz Fanon has famously recognized this necessary violence in *The Wretched of the Earth* (1961).[6] In literature, this
position echoes early "writing back" perspectives and Barthes' *écrivant*: explicit commitment, transparent, verbose, and exhaustive realism, the representation of fixed and non-contradictory identities, plots which evolve towards a collective *telos*, rather little concern about esthetics. So, while what I
call the *post-colonial* advocates for these logics of homogeneity and the
"either-or," the *postcolonial*, on the contrary, gives voice to the in-between,
the hybrid, the "undecidables" (Bauman 1990, 148); in other words, figures
who are at the same time near and far, same and different from dominant
identities, traditional and official representations.

Since my typology thus falls into *certain* modernist and postmodernist
tendencies, postures, discourses, and representations, a second step consists
of drawing on Ihab Hassan's attempt to provide the main socio-cultural and
esthetic articulations of postmodern texts. In a (now classic) essay, Hassan
suggested a list of eleven distinctive features of the nebula postmodernism
which can inform, at least partially, the *postcolonial* side of the contrastive
reading method here argued for. The list containing deconstructive and re-
constructive traits goes like this: 1) Indeterminacy, epistemological ambigu-
ities, ruptures, and displacements 2) Fragmentation and moving signifiers 3)
Decanonization 4) Deconstruction of the traditional subject and its supposed
profundity 5) Contestation of the modes of one's own representation 6) Irony

and its extensions 7) Hybridization 8) Carnivalization, heteroglossia, and polyphony 9) The performativity of the text and the need of the reader's participation 10) Constructionism 11) Non-religious immanence (Hassan 1986, 503–520). In a subsequent article, the late critic added other terms (auto-reflexivity, polychronic temporalities, etc.), explicitly differentiated between postmodernism (the cultural field) and postmodernity (the geopolitical condition and process), and observed: "Perhaps, after all, postmodernism can be 'defined' as a continuous inquiry into self-definition" (Hassan 2001). There are of course multiple perspectives on the protean field of postmodernism, and one needs to be careful when transferring these characteristics on the postcolonial writer: his contemporaneity cannot be reduced to mere epistemological demystification, deconstruction of form and language, ontological fragmentation, alienated identities, absurd ethos, ironic self-conscience, perpetual indetermination, and moving signifiers, associated with thinkers like Lyotard, Derrida, Baudrillard and others. Yet, numerous Mauritian texts with a more *postcolonial* tendency share some of these features: they do indeed demystify master-codes, delegitimize totalizing positions by addressing issues of minority, the margin, polyphony, and multiple spaces. And they inquire about self-definition by engaging with auto-deconstruction, irony, and metafiction.

Beyond the idea of a certain parallelism between the *post-colonial* and modernist logics on the one hand, the *postcolonial* and postmodern socio-esthetic traits on the other, it seems important to mention the intricate issue of the complex relationship between postmodernism and postcolonialism which has generated heated debates with key theorists in the field (Appiah, Hutcheon, Bhabha, Boehmer, Lazarus, Loomba, etc.). Despite terminological controversies about a possible reification and homogenization of the postcolonial world through the privileged status of thinkers living in diaspora—one can refer here to Aijaz Ahmad's and Arif Dirlik's polemics against an intelligentsia supposedly rendering postcolonialism into an agent of global capitalism (Ahmad 1992, Dirlik 1994)—the postcolonial shares with the postmodern essential aspects: both focus on difference, ex-centering, heterogeneity, and an interrogative and deconstructive mode of analysis; both are interested in historiography and politics of representation. Kwame Anthony Appiah argues that the prefixes "post" converge by their idea of the "beyond," signifying not only temporal succession but real transcendence: "the *post-* in postcolonial, like the *post-* in postmodern, is the *post-* of the space-clearing gesture"; it "challenges earlier legitimating narratives" (Appiah 1991, 348, 353). This idea is taken up by Bhabha who considers the "beyond" to be *the* trope to locate today's questions concerning culture (Bhabha 2008, 1–2).

However, these shared concerns and locations between the postmodern and the postcolonial are not articulated in the same way and the main difference undoubtedly concerns the idea of *agency*. Indeed, politics of identity cannot identify with the "typically postmodern truce" (Hutcheon 2005, 166), with its relativity, its "both/and" decisions and open-endedness. As Edward Said puts it, "the ahistorical weightlessness, consumerism, and spectacle of the new order" (Said 1994, 399) in much Western postmodernism, do less concern artists and intellectuals in places that are still involved with the modernist act, and that are still struggling with overcoming tradition and orthodox heritage. Put differently, the postcolonial text—whatever political role it may play—does not only represent a discursive contingency, as Elleke Boehmer strikingly notes:

> Postmodern and even postcolonial notions of meaning as arbitrary, or identity as provisional, are hardly relevant to the lives of those—women, Indigenous peoples, marginalized ethnic, class, and religious groups—for whom self-determination remains a political imperative. For them, the signifiers of home, self, past, far from representing instances of discursive contingency, stand for live and pressing issues. (Boehmer 2005, 242)

Shohat had similarly warned against postcolonialism's "ahistorical and universalizing deployments, and its potentially depoliticizing implications" (Shohat 1992, 242). With such evidence in mind, it becomes clear that the postcolonial text's signification, its social analysis and its concrete connection to the world cannot simply be dismissed in favor of purely formal and esthetic aspects. These debates have led, roughly speaking, to two critical directions within postcolonial theory which, while sharing the same premises, may diverge considerably: on the one hand, the more cosmopolitan, intellectual(ized) and often relativist site of migrant and transnational writers frequently living in the West and permanently running the risk of falling into the neo-orientalist and neo-exoticist trap (Huggan 2001); on the other, a more contextualizing approach centered around local and peripheral productions. Here lies of course the conflicting—and some may say incommensurable—antagonism between theoretical deconstruction and identity pragmatics, between "textualism" and materialism. Such a contrast between a postmodern postcolonialism (or even post-postcolonialism) and a more local or vernacular postcolonialism is meant to be reflected in the distinction between the *post-colonial* and the *postcolonial*; well knowing that the two poles stand in a complex relationship to each other and a theoretical pluralism enables to see fertile tensions and interactions between them. Bhabha—although generally considered to be one of the key figures in primarily theoretical postcolonialism—seems to touch precisely this aspect, by asserting that today's true postcolonial agency needs to go beyond the conventional polarity between theory and practice. Indeed, if the postcolonial intellectual project locates itself in the hybrid posture of the "beyond" with regard to all possible dichotomies, if it "resists the attempt at holistic forms of social explanation" (Bhabha 2008, 248), this transgresses both postmodernism's cultural pluralism or relativism and exclusivist national or collective paradigms.

In this sense, Bhabha's postcolonial reading of the nation and his set of oppositions between "the pedagogical" and "the performative" can be mobilized as yet another complementary tool for my contrastive reading method. Drawing on Benedict Anderson's "imagined communities" and inspired by Derrida for the notion of "DissemiNation," the critic argues against the idea of a unified and unitary national culture and observes, on the contrary, increasing markers of cultural difference and heterogeneity in the nation.[7] He sees the supposed national linearity and homogeneity as being troubled by minority discourse, cultural liminality, and otherness: an otherness residing in the people's identity itself. In other words: the *pedagogical* claim for fixed identities and organic totality is more than ever challenged by the *performative* real. In the case of multicultural and creolized Mauritius, where any mono-ethnic national narration seems impossible, we need to shift from *nation* to *community* or *collective identity*. For if ethnicizing policies seem impossible on the level of the nation—in the same way that nativist claims in an island without indigenous population are untenable—these policies operate *within* the nation. Indeed, official "Unity in diversity" discourses rely on the *pedagogical* vision of ethnically homogeneous and coherent groups, internally totalizing historicity and fixed ideas of otherness. Hybridity, historic discontinuity, plural solidarities and social creolization, which are central parts of the island society's *performative* reality, tend to be relegated to the margin of the model "Rainbow nation."

A final analogy may come from the common ground between postcolonialism and feminism, as well as resemblances in the evolutions of these disciplines/movements. It is symptomatic that McClintock has based her call to diversify the notion of "post-colonial" on the example of the discredit brought upon the category of *the* universal woman (McClintock 1992, 86). Similarly, Bhabha acknowledges the influence of Kristeva's idea of female temporality on his postcolonial philosophy and psychology (Bhabha 2008, 219 *sq.*). Since postcolonialism and feminism can operate similar strategies in order to assert themselves within dominant and hegemonic discourse, one may argue for a conceptual correspondence between the *"post-colonial"*-"postcolonial" reference frame on the one hand, the contrast between identitarian feminist approaches and new (post)feminist tendencies on the other. More precisely, this analogy can be seen with Kristeva's article "Women's Time" where both egalitarian and differentialist feminist conceptions are rejected in favor of alternative temporalities. The critic dismisses universalist approaches and the idea of an exclusive female specificity in order to proclaim a new signifying space where the "singularity of each woman, and beyond this, her multiplicities, her plural languages" (Kristeva 1997, 214) can unfold. Such a theory, which takes into account the potentials of a fluid (postmodern) subjectivity while supporting social and ethical questions, can arguably inform tendencies within the postcolonial field. The *post-colonial* tendency of the proposed reading method appears here first and foremost concerned by collective stances—be they egalitarian or differentialist— whereas the *postcolonial* pole focuses on more individual manifestations of otherness.

These reflections then converge into the critical typology of the *post-colonial* and the *postcolonial*, developed in order to interpret current novel production in Mauritius, its different concepts of time and space/place, its representations of and discourses on *self* and *other*, its esthetic and narrative identities. A more precise look at some concrete examples shall illustrate these thoughts.

## EXAMPLES FROM THE MAURITIAN NOVEL PRODUCTION

Not surprisingly, certain Mauritian authors thematize the multiple and conflicting pasts of the island. Thus, the subject of Indian indentureship comes up in various texts about the coolies' odyssey from the subcontinent to the island. *The Changing Pattern* (1995) by Bhageeruthy Gopaul, *Beaux Songes* (1999) by Nando Bodha, *The Snake Spirit* (2002) by Chaya Parmessur or *That Others Might Live* (1976) by Deepchand Beeharry are such memorialist endeavours which take up the important role of filling in the subaltern gaps in traditional literary representation. Yet, a closer look reveals that they often do not go beyond mystifications of a purely ethnicized memory: they provide brave narratives of migration or nostalgic accounts of Indo-Mauritian life with its pedagogies of unbroken filiations. Such victimizing or idealizing discourses are obstacles for historical dialogue and intercultural widening of horizons (Arnold 2012). The rhetoric of pathos and the emotive subjectivity they frequently deploy draw on collective emotions, which is prone to reduce the plurality of cultural values and may even flirt with ideological manipulation (Rinn 2008). On the contrary, Nathacha Appanah's novel *Les Rochers de Poudre d'Or* (2003), for example, transgresses such conventional narratives of originary and initial subjectivities. Her polyphonic fiction abandons the idea of glorification and heroic quest in unity. She gives the *kala pani* paradigm a more multifaceted and also feminine touch and provides a complex comparison between indenture and slavery. Ananda Devi, in the novel *Le Voile de Draupadi* (1993), goes even further by deconstructing the traditional diasporic narrative and demystifying its patriarchal and religious foundations in favor of contemporary subaltern voices. Her transgressive protagonist violently defies the claims of monolithic ancestry and points towards an intercultural opening-up. With these indenture novels and their opposing views on origins, filiation, sacredness, convention, and the individual, the contrast between what is called *post-colonial* and *postcolonial* can clearly be seen.

Another example comes from the text *Terre d'orages* (2003) by Serge Ng Tat Chung which, strikingly, is the only contemporary novel representing the period of slavery in Mauritius. However, close analysis of the work shows again that beyond its undeniable merit to speak for the absent African voices in literary discourse (Prabhu 2005), and beyond the fact that it avoids the ethnicizing positions of the indenture novels, it remains stuck in a blissful conciliatory perspective of the past which portrays a happy multiculturalism perfectly in line with official representations of the subject (Arnold 2014). On the contrary, in *Le Silence des Chagos* (2005) by Shenaz Patel or *Ceux qu'on jette à la mer* (2001) by Carl de Souza, we find more contemporary plots behind which unveils subtly the paradigm of slave deportation (Magdelaine-Andrianjafitrimo 2008). Patel's text is particularly interesting insofar as, in order to emancipate the oppressed protagonists, it plays with the idea of "strategic essentialism"—the recognition that the leveling of differences is necessary to secure political agency (Spivak 1987, 205)—while at the same time investing the notion of "multidirectional memory" (Rothberg 2009). Put differently, the novel advocates both for one group's affirmation of identity and for the resonance of the "the trace of the other" (Spivak 1999, 198). Concerning racial relations under colonialism, one equally observes diverging perspectives. Whereas Marie-Thérèse Humbert, in *À l'autre bout de moi* (1979), and Julia Blackburn, in *The Book of Colour* (1995), provide a complex discussion about colonial *métissage* through the figure of the light-skinned Creole (*mulâtre*) and the subversion of ethno-racial taboos, other texts—such as *La Brûlure* (2003) by Renée Asgarally—idealize on the contrary intercultural questions and romanticize interethnic transgressions.

One could also refer to the novels of Lindsey Collen, especially *There Is a Tide* (1991), *The Rape of Sita* (1993), and *Getting Rid of It* (1997). Through their multiple commitments for gender and racial identities, their complex representations of history and present as well as their elaborated, often hybrid, style and esthetics, these texts reflect a truly emancipated *postcolonial* position. But one can also frequently observe rather radical feminist and (neo-)Marxist didactics in them which clearly show that the author cannot be counted among the cosmopolitan postmodern postcolonialists. With regard to Collen's multifaceted work, which is not devoid of its own internal contradictions, Kristeva's idea of "multiple temporalities" co-existing at the same time comes to mind. One of the Mauritian writers who seems to correspond to this perspective of the "cosmopolitan postmodern postcolonialist" is Amal Sewtohul. His novels which heavily draw on Rushdie's *bricolage*-esthetics—especially *Les voyages et aventures de Sanjay* (2009)—deal with the motive of migration, hybridity, stylistic exuberance and self-irony (Arnold 2011). While these texts may at moments appear

elitist and hermetic, and while more than often the idea of postcolonial exoticism becomes palpable, they arguably express a most complex contemporaneity.[8] In terms of hybridity, Ananda Devi's novels—notably *Moi,
l'interdite* (2000) and *La Vie de Joséphin le fou* (2003)—do figure as
prominent examples for a negative and pessimistic interpretation of the
concept. Her transgressive texts can "provide a political space to articulate such culturally hybrid social identities" (Bhabha 2008, 359). In general, with the Indo-Mauritian author it seems clear that "marginality . . .
became an unprecedented source of creative energy" (Ashcroft et al.
2005, 12). Her fiction is indeed filled with ostracized, queer, erratic, and
rejected characters for whom (self)violence certainly often seems the only
way of affirmation, but whose uncanny presence permits to ask unpleasant
questions which prove to be decisive to discuss identity, justice, and democ-
racy in its contemporary plurality. A final—quite "extreme"—example
would be Devi's exploration of the arctic in her short story "Bleu glace"
(2007), an investment on the antipodes of her more usual island chronotopos.
Interestingly, the general opening up of spaces and referential universes in
contemporary Mauritian fiction echoes here literally with the entry of new
conceptual and geographical territory in the theoretical debate, such as recent
attempts at "decolonizing the Arctic" (Huggan 2015).

    This brief overview shows that when asking the following questions—
How do the writers imagine their island space? How do they depict the
relationship between and within communities? How do they think racial,
gender, and social identity construction? How do they deal with history and
memory? How do they perceive ambivalent, moving, and transitory phenomena in society? What is their attitude toward tradition, convention, and the
*doxa*?—the positions of the *post-colonial* and the *postcolonial* can provide
different answers. *Postcolonial* Mauritian texts are then the manifestation
that the hybridity of literary and social discourse has become one of the
leitmotifs of our contemporary world. Not only is their high degree of inter-
textuality remarkable, but contrary to the *post-colonial* claims about homogenous and unitary belonging—in terms of community, religion, history, patriarchy . . . —they seem to have moved on to the "next" stage. It is here that
one observes textual innovation where the nation is examined and questioned
from the perspective of the margins, ambiguous interstices, friction, and
discontinuity. These novels may thus draw on postmodern modes and invest
original styles and themes: hybridity, metafiction, re-imagining former literary paradigms, break with tradition mimesis (Magdelaine-Andrianjafitrimo
2004), "anti-tropicalization" (Arnold 2014), etc. Clearly, the different productions within the Mauritian literary field/space do not evolve at the same
pace. But the examples reveal as well that a clear-cut contrastive reading
between *post-colonial* and *postcolonial* fiction is frequently not possible and

that we are dealing with unstable poles on some kind of continuum, transitions, and penetrable spheres.

## CONCLUDING THOUGHTS

It is certain that whatever internal nuance one may find within the notion of postcoloniality, most postcolonial writing—through its new literary and linguistic codes, its new modes of representation, and its complex position within (inter)national markets—engages a (more or less subtle) cultural and political critique in order to endorse otherness, focus on "peripheral" identity, and emancipate past and present minority and subaltern groups. Yet postcolonial studies' various legacies (Marxist criticism, cultural studies, deconstruction . . .) and present influences (globalization, transnationalism . . .) do not translate equally—quite far from it—in Mauritian literature. Thus, in the contrastive reading method, with regard to the construction and representation of identities, and socio-ethnic positioning, the *post-colonial* Mauritian texts tend to fall into dialectics of *same* and *other* which fail to acknowledge the complexity of reality. Even though they often invest necessary sites of engagement—to resist injustice, reaffirm offended identities, reconstruct missing memory, etc.—they are prone to homogenize collective identities, and to omit hybrid realities and stakes concerning the individual. These fictions operate through clearly defined, stable, voluntarist or even heroic characters who are frequently representative of a larger unit. Such figures bear coherent worldviews and unwavering projects, rely on traditional belief or myth; they tend to romanticize the past and depict the island under conformist, politically correct or folkloric traits. The *post-colonial* texts may remain stuck in conventional ethnographical figurations with their cultural inventories, recurrent themes, often didactic stances, frequent use of pathos, and Bhabha's idea of the "pedagogical." Their "contrapuntal" or "writing back" perspectives do only concern colonial or Western reference frames; they only seldom destabilize the *doxa* and question or jeopardize power relations in nowadays society.

On the other hand, we find *postcolonial* texts with more contemporary, emancipated, and postmodern directions and textures, in which universal configurations of social explanation and collective standpoints have seriously lost their efficiency. These texts position themselves, more or less explicitly, as "counter-narratives"[9] in relation to the identity fixation operated by the official discourse of the nation. They imagine the island's modernity by taking into consideration its irremediably heterogeneous space as well as the individuals with their plural, but potentially fragmented belonging. The *post-colonial* text unsettles restrictive classifications and breaks with traditional representations of the island in favor of more flexible references and the idea of transitions instead of oppositions—Nietzsche's aphorism about the "habit of contrasts"[10] comes to mind. While these fictions do not deny commitment—deploying it, however, with more subtlety—they go beyond monological claims in order to focus on the individual's multiple, but also troubled and marginal identity as well as new (and often transgressive) representations of the island. If the *postcolonial* text, deconstructs Manichean logics and accepts or even valorizes figures of difference, mixture, and mobility, it does, however, not fall into the trap of postmodern indetermination, nor celebrate blindly a blissful hybridity. Not only does it subscribe to Bhabha's idea of the *performative*, but it also reminds of Barthes's vision of *true* fiction: fiction that less aims at telling truths but introduces doubt and ambiguity into our certainties. Thus, in a *postcolonial* scenography, looking back in time and space goes beyond paralyzing nostalgia or lament; past and present interact by reading one through the prism of the other so to invest history as a constructive and enabling, yet critical tool in the enunciative temporality of the text.

On the level of discourse and narration, the *post-colonial* affirmation of identity often translates by a relatively conventional esthetics somewhat corresponding to the characteristics of Barthes's *écrivant*: (documentary) realism, description, Olympic third-person narration, chronology, simple focalization, etc. It comes in the shape of testimony, with a clear explanation of the world and sometimes—but not systematically—commitment to a cause or emotive rhetoric. In other words, the *post-colonial* regime generally provides a "position expressed without ambiguity."[11] The *postcolonial* text, on the contrary, often brings along innovation, or even subversion of discourse and genre: stylistic transgression, code switching, a-chronology, fragmentation, polyphonic focalization, emphasis on psychology and the interior world, sometimes stylistic exuberance. *Postcolonial* fiction tends to operate a friction between languages and destabilizes the codifications of conventional literary genre, thus reflecting more appropriately the complexity of the island society. But one can also find short forms, stark and minimalist styles and esthetics like those designated by the idea of the "writing degree zero" (Barthes 1953), which are the complete opposite of the newly canonized neo-exoticisms. Barlen Pyamootoo's *Bénarès* (1999) and *Le Tour de Babylone* (2002), but also Bertrand de Robillard's *L'homme qui penche* (2003) and *Une interminable distraction au monde* (2011), which look like a contemporary variety of the Nouveau Roman paradigm, are striking examples of such esthetic and narrative rupture; they are difficult to locate within new Francophone and transnational conventions. This being said, the *postcolonial* novel adheres more to innovation, textual work and the question of "How to write?" of Barthes's *écrivain* without being reduced to it.

Interestingly, in the contemporary Mauritian novel, the separation between the *post-colonial* and the *postcolonial* goes often—but not exclusively—along with the linguistic dividing line English-French as well as a generational transition. The discursive and thematic renewal since the mid-1990s do indeed mostly concern the island's fiction written in French. Besides, the two tendencies can generally be found in different circles of editing and reception. An essential aspect in this discussion then also concerns the question of the Mauritian literary field and its place in the Francophone and Anglophone "literary system" (Halen 2001, 2003) or, more generally, in the "world republic of letters" (Casanova 1999). Very often—at least with regard to style—the question whether an author is published in the European (or Western) metropolitan "centers" or elsewhere does directly inform the critical reading method this chapter is putting forward, although notable exceptions exist.[12] And quite evidently, this topological discussion opens up the tricky issue of postcolonial exoticism (Huggan 2001) and the controversial notion of *authenticity* (Jourde 2001); let alone the ultimate question of each reader's and critic's position.

It needs to be underlined that the *post-colonial* texts shall by no means be discredited or relegated to the past: their merit lies in the fact that they often introduce to us literature figures who have traditionally been absent, and their perspectives of identity can reveal a lot about social discourses, values, and worldviews. Albeit their possibly lesser literary quality, they do not have to be ruled out in the negotiation of identities and imaginary worlds. However, I argue that the *postcolonial* vision suggests a more creative, innovative, and daring perspective to critically reflect upon our contemporary times. It translates better postcolonialism's pivotal ideas of *difference* and *identities in movement*, withstands more successfully the temptation of essentialist fixation, and inquires further into the question "how newness enters the world" (Bhabha 2008, 303–337). It shows that dominant representations in (and of) the island have to take into account the constructed dimension of belonging, to see Mauritian society as it is, that is to say at the same time diasporic and ethnically fractured as profoundly hybrid and creolized. It thus tends to what one could consider to be a truly emancipated postcolonial scenography where cultural difference, past and present are dealt with in all their complexity. The suggested typology is not meant to be a rigid corset forced upon a most diverse corpus. It is aware of the singularities of each author and text, it adheres to the idea of "discrepant experiences" (Said 1994, 36) which have to lie at the heart of any comparative (postcolonial) study, and it knows about the abusive schematization of terms such as "postmodern postcolonialist" (Spivak 1999, 361). Not only is what is here called *post-colonial* and *postcolonial* neither categorical nor static; the two are the poles of a mobile "grid" within which exist evident oscillations, convergences, and transitions. This reading method may thus permit to outline and to understand certain recurrent features in the different temporalities and heterogeneities of the emerging literary field of Mauritius, as well as other postcolonial spaces.

## NOTES

1. This is a modified version of the article "Between Post-colonial and Postcolonial: A Reading Proposal through and for the Contemporary Novel Production of Mauritius (and Beyond)," published in *Pensée, pratiques et poétiques postcoloniales contemporaines: Monde atlantique et océan Indien*, edited by Rodolphe Solbiac, 113–140, Paris: L'Harmattan, 2018.
2. *Cf.* "creuser la surface des labels" (Joubert 2014, 7). All translations are mine.
3. I borrow the term "stratum" from Patricia Donatien (2015) who argues that the postcolonial in different historical stages (*étapes*) in the Caribbean is structured in various strata or levels (*strates*).
4. Bauman, Zygmunt, "From pilgrim to tourist; or A short story of identity," in *Questions of Cultural Identity*, ed. Stuart Hall, and Paul Du Gay (London: Sage, 1996), 18. Quoted by Eriksen (2002, 143).
5. *Cf.* "Under the rubric 'the discourse of modernity', [one should not] reduce a complex and diverse historical moment, with varied national genealogies and different institutional practices into a singular shibboleth—be it the 'idea' of Reason, Historicism, Progress—for the convenience of postmodern literary theory" (Bhabha 2008, 342).
6. *Cf.* for example his observation, with regard to the question of nationalist struggle, about an inevitable "brutality and a contempt for subtleties and individual cases" (Fanon 2002, 140).
7. *Cf.* "a space that is *internally* marked by cultural difference and the heterogeneous histories of contending peoples, antagonistic authorities, and tense cultural locations" (Bhabha 2008, 299).
8. In his more recent fiction—*Made in Mauritius* (2012) and *A la dérive* (2014)—Sewtohul seems to have reduced the somewhat excessive and oneiric dimension of his narrative, while maintaining his leitmotifs of interculturality, mobility, and transnationalism.
9. *Cf.* "Counter-narratives of the nation that continually evoke and erase its totalizing boundaries—both actual and conceptual—disturb those ideological manoeuvres through which 'imagined communities' are given essentialist identities" (Bhabha 2003, 300).
10. *Cf.* "The Habit of Contrasts—Superficial, inexact observation sees contrasts everywhere in nature (for instance, "hot and cold"), where there are no contrasts, only *differences of degree*. This bad habit has induced us to try to understand and interpret even the inner nature, the intellectual and moral world, in accordance with such contrasts. An infinite amount of cruelty, arrogance, harshness, estrangement, and coldness has entered into human emotion, because men imagined they saw contrasts where there were only transitions" (Nietzsche 2006, 388, my italics).
11. *Cf.* "prise de position formulée sans ambiguïté" (Mouralis 1975, 185).
12. One might think here about Lindsey Collen's or Amal Sewtohul's locally published novels, as well as Brigitte Masson's *Le chant de l'aube qui s'éveille* (2012), a hybrid narrative with a straightforward political and transcultural stance, while at the same time original in stylistic and esthetic terms.

## BIBLIOGRAPHY

Ahmad, Aijaz. *In Theory: Classes, Nations, Literatures*. London: Verso, 1992.
Appanah, Nathacha. *Les Rochers de Poudre d'Or*. Paris: Gallimard, coll. "Continents noirs," 2003.
Appiah, Kwame Anthony. "Is the Post- in Postmodernism the Post- in Postcolonial?" *Critical Inquiry* 17 (1991): 336–357.
Arnold, Markus. *La littérature mauricienne contemporaine: Un espace de création postcolonial entre revendications identitaires et ouvertures interculturelles*. Berlin: Lit, 2017.

————. "Les univers étranges, intimes et violents de l'auteur mauricien Carl de Souza: un cas d'anti-tropicalisation du roman." *Les Lettres Romanes* 68, no. 1–2 (2014): 73–101.
————. "Coming to terms with the past? The controversial issue of slavery in contemporary Mauritian fiction." *Journal of Romance Studies* 14, no. 2 (2014): 5–19.
————. "'Undergoing wonderful sea changes'? Indian migration in contemporary Mauritian fiction in English between ethnicisation and intercultural ideals." *Journal of Mauritian Studies* 6, no. 2 (2012): 33–66.
————. "Cosmopolitan Visions and Odysseys of Memory: Identity Twists in the Writing of Mauritian Author Amal Sewtohul." In *Hybridity: Forms and Figures in Literature and the Visual Arts*, edited by Vanessa Guignery, Catherine Pesso-Miquel, and François Specq, 332–343. Newcastle upon Tyne: Cambridge Scholars, 2011.
Asgarally, Renée. *La Brûlure*. Péreybère (Mauritius): Éditions Mascarena, 2003.
Ashcroft, Bill. "Postcolonial Utopianism." *The Future of Postcolonial Studies*, edited by Chantal Zabus, 235–253. London; New York: Routledge, 2015.
Ashcroft, Bill, Gareth Griffith, and Helen Tiffin. *The Empire Writes Back*. London; New York: Routledge, 2005 [1989].
Barthes, Roland. *Le degré zéro de l'écriture, suivi de Nouveaux essais critiques*. Paris: Seuil, 1972 [1953].
————. "Écrivains et écrivants." In *Essais critiques*, 147–154. Paris: Seuil, coll. "Tel quel," 1964.
Bauman, Zygmunt. "Modernity and Ambivalence." *Theory, Culture & Society* 7, no. 2–3 (1990): 143–169.
————. "The Making and Unmaking of Strangers." In *Debating Cultural Hybridity: Multi-Cultural Identities and the Politics of Anti-Racism*, edited by Pnina Werbner and Tariq Modood, 46–57. London: ZED Books Ltd., 1997.
Beeharry, Deepchand. *That Others Might Live. A Novel on the Tragic Life of Early Indian Immigrants in Mauritius*. Delhi: Natraj Prakashan, 1998 [1976].
Bhabha, Homi, ed. *Nation and Narration*. London; New York: Routledge, 2003 [1990].
Bhabha, Homi. *The Location of Culture*. London; New York: Routledge, 2008 [1994].
Blackburn, Julia. *The Book of Colour*. London: Jonathan Cape, 1995.
Bodha, Nando. *Beaux Songes*. Bénarès (Mauritius): Editions Bénarès, 1999.
Boehmer, Elleke. *Colonial and Postcolonial Literature*. Oxford: Oxford University Press, 2005 [1995].
Bonn, Charles. "Scénographie postcoloniale et ambiguïté tragique dans la littérature algérienne de langue française, ou: pour en finir avec un discours binaire." (2006): http://www.limag.refer.org/Textes/Bonn/2006Tipasa.pdf [Accessed: April 2018].
————. "Scénographie postcoloniale et 'définition forte de l'espace d'énonciation' dans le roman maghrébin." In *Les études littéraires francophones: État des lieux*, edited by Jean-Marc Moura, and Lieven D'Hulst. 127–140. Lille: Presses de l'université de Lille 3, 2003.
Casanova, Pascale. *La république mondiale des lettres*. Paris: Seuil, coll. "Points essais," 2008 [1999].
Clifford, James. *Routes: Travel and Translation in the Late Twentieth Century*. Cambridge, MA; London: Harvard University Press, 1997.
Collen, Lindsey. *There Is a Tide*. Grand River North West (Mauritius): Ledikasyon pu Travayer, 1991.
————. *The Rape of Sita*. London: Bloomsbury, 1993.
————. *Getting Rid of It*. London: Granta, 1997.
De Robillard, Bertrand. *L'homme qui penche*. Paris: Éditions de l'Olivier, 2003.
————. *Une interminable distraction au monde*. Paris: Éditions de l'Olivier, 2011.
De Souza, Carl. *Ceux qu'on jette à la mer*. Paris: Éditions de l'Olivier, 2001.
Devi, Ananda. "Bleu glace." In *Nouvelles de l'île Maurice*, 45–69. Paris: Magellan & Cie, coll. "Miniatures," 2007.
————. *La Vie de Joséphin le fou*. Paris: Gallimard, coll. "Continents noirs," 2003.
————. *Moi, l'interdite*. Paris: Dapper, 2000.
————. *Le Voile de Draupadi*. Vacoas (Mauritius): Éditions Le Printemps, 1993.

Dirlik, Arif. "The Postcolonial Aura: Third World Criticism in the Age of Global Capitalism." *Critical Inquiry* 20, no. 2 (Winter 1994): 328–356.

Donatien, Patricia. "De la validité d'une esthétique postcoloniale dans la Caraïbe du 21e siècle." Paper at International Conference "Qu'est-ce-que la pensée postcoloniale? ¿Que es el pensamiento postcolonial? What is Postcolonial Thought?" University of the Antilles, Martinique, November 23–25, 2015.

Douglas, Mary. *Purity and Danger: An Analysis of Concepts of Pollution and Taboo*. London; New York: Routledge, 2007 [1966].

Eriksen, Thomas Hylland. *Ethnicity and Nationalism*. London: Pluto Press, 2002 [1993].

Fanon, Frantz. *Les Damnés de la Terre*. Paris: La Découverte, coll. "Poche," 2002 [1961].

Gilroy, Paul. *The Black Atlantic: Modernity and Double Consciousness*. Cambridge, MA: Harvard University Press, 1993.

Gopaul, Bhageeruthy. *The Changing Pattern*. Rose Hill (Mauritius): Éditions de l'océan Indien, 1995.

Halen, Pierre. "Notes pour une topologie institutionnelle du système littéraire francophone." In *Littératures et sociétés africaines: Regards comparatistes et perspectives interculturelles. Mélanges offerts à János Riesz à l'occasion de son soixantième anniversaire*, edited by Papa Samba Diop and Hans-Jürgen Lüsebrink, 55–67. Tübingen: Narr, 2001.

———. "Le 'système littéraire francophone': quelques réflexions complémentaires." In *Les études littéraires francophones: État des lieux*, edited by Jean-Marc Moura and Lieven d'Hulst, 25–37. Lille: Presses de l'université de Lille 3, 2003.

Hassan, Ihab. "Pluralism in Postmodern Perspective." *Critical Inquiry* 12, no. 3 (Spring 1986): 503–520.

———. "From Postmodernism to Postmodernity: The Local/Global Context." *Philosophy and Literature* 25, no. 1 (2001): 1–13. Project MUSE.

Huggan, Graham. "Notes on the Postcolonial Arctic." In *The Future of Postcolonial Studies*, edited by Chantal Zabus, 130–143. London; New York: Routledge, 2015.

———. *The Postcolonial Exotic: Marketing the Margins*. London; New York: Routledge, 2001.

Humbert, Marie-Thérèse. *À l'autre bout de moi*. Paris: Stock, 1979.

Hutcheon, Linda. *The Politics of Postmodernism*. London; New York: Routledge, 2005 [1989].

Joubert, Claire, ed. *Le postcolonial comparé: anglophonie, francophonie*. Paris: Presses Universitaires de Vincennes, coll. "Littérature Hors Frontière," 2014.

Jourde, Pierre. *Littérature et authenticité. Le réel, le neutre, la fiction*. Paris: L'esprit des péninsules, 2005 [2001].

Kristeva, Julia. "Women's Time." In *The Feminist Reader: Essays in Gender and the Politics of Literary Criticism*, edited by Catherine Belsey and Jane Moore, 197–218. Macmillan Press: London, 1997 [1989].

Lazarus, Neil. *The Postcolonial Unconscious*, Cambridge: Cambridge University Press, 2011.

Le Bris, Michel, and Jean Rouaud, eds. *Pour une littérature-monde*. Paris: Gallimard, 2007.

Loomba, Ania. *Colonialism/Postcolonialism*. London; New York: Routledge, coll. "the new critical idiom," 2008 [1998].

Magdelaine-Andrianjafitrimo, Valérie. "Ethnicisation ou créolisation? Le paradigme de la traite dans quelques romans francophones mauriciens contemporains." *e-France: an on-line journal of French Studies* 2 (2008): 100–115.

——— . "Le 'désancrage' et la déréalisation de l'écriture chez trois écrivains mauriciens, Ananda Devi, Carl de Souza, Barlen Pyamootoo." In *L'Entredire francophone*, edited by Martine Mathieu-Job, 67–100. Bordeaux: Presses Universitaires de Bordeaux, 2004.

Maingueneau, Dominique. *Le contexte de l'oeuvre littéraire. Énonciation, écrivain, société*. Paris: Dunod, 1993.

Masson, Brigitte. *Le chant de l'aube qui s'éveille*. Mauritius: La Maison des Mécènes, 2012.

McClintock, Anne. "The Angel of Progress: Pitfalls of the Term 'Post-Colonialism.'" *Social Text* 31–32 (1992): 84–98.

Moura, Jean-Marc. *Littératures francophones et théorie postcoloniale*. Paris: PUF, 1999.

Mouralis, Bernard. *Les contre-littératures*. Paris: PUF, coll. "sup," 1975.

Ng Tat Chung, Serge. *Terre d'orages*. Port Louis: Centre Nelson Mandela pour la Culture Africaine, 2003.

Nietzsche, Friedrich. *Human, All-Too-Human: Parts One and Two*. Mineola, New York: Dover Publications, 2006 [1880].

Parmessur, Chaya. *The Snake Spirit—Part 1: The Fire Giver*. Bloomington (US): X-libris, 2002.

Patel, Shenaz. *Le Silence des Chagos*. Paris: Éditions de l'Olivier, 2005.

Prabhu, Anjali. "Representation in Mauritius: Who Speaks for African Pasts?" *International Journal of Francophone Studies* 8, no. 2 (2005): 183–197.

Pyamootoo, Barlen. *Bénarès*. Paris: Éditions de l'Olivier, 1999.

———. *Le Tour de Babylone*. Paris: Éditions de l'Olivier, 2002.

Rinn, Michael, ed. *Émotions et discours. L'usage des passions dans la langue*. Rennes: Presses Universitaires de Rennes, coll. "Interférences," 2008.

Rothberg, Michael. *Multidirectional Memory: Remembering the Holocaust in the Age of Decolonization*. Stanford: Stanford University Press, 2009.

Rushdie, Salman. "'Commonwealth Literature' does not exist." In *Imaginary Homelands: Essays and Criticism 1981–1991*. 61–70. London: Granta & Penguin, 1991.

Said, Edward. *Culture and Imperialism*. London: Vintage, 1994 [1993].

Sewtohul, Amal. *Les voyages et aventures de Sanjay, explorateur mauricien des Anciens Mondes*. Paris: Gallimard, coll. "Continents noirs," 2009.

———. *Made in Mauritius*. Paris: Gallimard, coll. "Continents noirs," 2012.

———. *A la dérive*. Pamplemousses (Mauritius): Pamplemousses Editions, 2014.

Shohat, Ella, "Notes on the 'Post-Colonial.'" *Social Text* 31–32 (1992): 99–113.

Slemon, Stephen. "The Scramble for Post-colonialism." In *De-Scribing Empire: Post-Colonialism and Textuality*, edited by Chris Tiffin and Alan Lawson, 15–32. London; New York: Routledge, 1994.

Spivak, Gayatri Chakravorty. *Death of a Discipline*. New York: Columbia University Press, 2003.

———. *A Critique of Postcolonial Reason: Toward a History of the Vanishing Present*. Cambridge, MA; London: Harvard University Press, 1999.

———. *In Other Worlds: Essays in Cultural Politics*. London: Taylor & Francis, 1987.

Zabus, Chantal, ed. *The Future of Postcolonial Studies*. London; New York: Routledge, 2015.

## Chapter Four

# "I'm a believer in the dance of change"

*Metamorphosis and Mutation in Keri Hulme's*
*Short Fiction*

## Melanie Otto

Keri Hulme is best known for her Booker Prize–winning novel *The Bone People* (1984), which became an instant bestseller and has remained one of the most successful novels written by an author with Maori heritage. The book occupies a key position in New Zealand literature and was the first novel by a Maori writer to win the Booker Prize, bringing Maori writing to international attention. *The Bone People* envisions a bicultural future for New Zealand in which, in Hulme's own words, everyone has "lost out by Maori people not being spiritually fully alive" (Hall 1984, 132). As a result of its prominent literary and cultural position, critical responses to the novel have largely dominated Hulme scholarship to date. Her two collections of short fiction, *Te Kaihau/The Windeater* (1986) and *Stonefish* (2004), have received much less critical attention, even though her engagement with New Zealand's changing perceptions of biculturalism, ecology, and gender are as radical, if not more so, as they are in her novel.

In conjunction with her self-professed interest in science fiction, Hulme's work explores the question of what makes us human and how a changing environment impacts on the development of human culture in the Pacific region. Environmentalism is, in fact, a concern that pervades all of her work. Many of her texts respond to such issues as food safety, global warming, and the negative effects of tourism and globalization on the fragile environments of the South Pacific. At the same time, Hulme's environmentalism can be placed in the context of indigenous conservationism, which has long been central to Pacific island life: the subsistence communities of the South Pacific have traditionally relied on the preservation of natural resources for their survival (Keown 2007, 89). In *Homeplaces* (1989), Hulme stresses the need to guard against overfishing and, like her Maori ancestors, observes the appropriate seasons, which dovetails with modern, state-regulated as well as international conservationism (Hulme 1989, 114–15). She also cautions against greed in the context of conservation, while elevating moderation to a spiritual level: "Why spoil the holiness of a dream-catch come true? Why ruin perfection with greed?" (Hulme 1989, 110). A certain concern for conservation is, therefore, at the heart of Hulme's environmentalism. However, her interest in the empowering aspects of mutant life-forms that are the product of climate change, evolution, or of bio-technological engineering adds a future-orientated dimension to her understanding of culture and ecology.

"I'm a believer in the dance of change," Hulme tells us in *Homeplaces*, her essays on the three New Zealand coasts central to her life: Okarito, Moeraki, and Rakiura (Hulme 1989, 64). In the first instance, this comment refers to the changing coastal environment of Moeraki, the "homeplace" most closely associated with Hulme's family history (it appears as Moerangi beach in *The Bone People*): "The sea gives, and the sea takes away, and if it breaks up Tikoraki and devastates the cribs, even the beloved Black Bach that I look after . . . well, so be it" (Hulme 1989, 64).[1] Tikoraki is an area of coastal rock that at the time of Hulme's writing of *Homeplaces* had begun to be eroded by the sea. While some residents of Moeraki voiced the need for conservation, Hulme herself has rejected this in favor of embracing change and adapting to the rhythm of the environment (Hulme 1989, 64). In the same book, she reflects on her own observations of mutation. On her daily walks around Okarito, the "homeplace" where she has built her Octagon house, she passes a "mutant rata vine":

> By the bridge corner, I see there are still some flowers on the mutant rata vine. That thing hasn't stopped producing blossoms for nearly two years, and it's beginning to worry me. Is it a good tohu, a good sign that it continues to flourish when the winters have been harsh, and all normal rata vines cease flowering in May or June at latest? Or an omen that the world is warping? (Hulme 1989, 18)

Hulme leaves these questions unanswered, partly because they are unanswerable but also because change, such as the ebb and flow of the tide, seasonal rainfall, and the migration of animals, is part of the coastal regions not just of New Zealand but the world at large.

In looking towards the future, Hulme's writing differs from more familiar postcolonial debates in that it engages not only with New Zealand's colonial past and how this affects its postcolonial present, but it also imagines an alternative future for the Pacific region in a way that is in conversation with debates in the field of postcolonial science fiction.[2] Combining environmental issues and speculative fiction, Hulme's two collections of short prose explore concepts such as hybridity and migration from a fresh and unusual perspective. In this way, both *Te Kaihau/The Windeater* and *Stonefish* tackle the question of how changing environments, ecological, technological, and social, impact on human culture in New Zealand and the South Pacific. As such, Hulme's ruminations about mutation and metamorphosis extend into debates around the future of biculturalism, the official term used to refer to the cultural relations between Maori and Pakeha (white settler) communities in New Zealand.

Large-scale settlement of the islands of New Zealand by Europeans began in the first decades of the nineteenth century, culminating in the Treaty of Waitangi, signed on February 6, 1840, by representatives of the British Crown and around 500 Maori chiefs from North Island. Drawn up in English and Maori, the Treaty proclaimed to regulate governance of the colony and protect land rights of both white settler and Maori communities. Yet, the two language versions differed significantly in meaning, especially in their understanding of the word "sovereignty," which was translated into Maori as "kawanatanga," meaning "governance" (*New Zealand History* 2014). In addition, increased immigration from Europe demanded more land for settlement, which in the early decades of the nineteenth century was largely situated in coastal areas. European advancement into the interior of North Island between the 1840s and 1870s resulted in a series of conflicts, the so-called New Zealand Wars, between Maori and Crown and colonial forces. Land captured or confiscated from Maori during and after the wars was taken in breach of the Treaty, marking the beginning of a fraught history of protests and grievances between Maori and Pakeha communities (Keenan 2017).

Maori have continued to look to the Treaty for rights and remedies relating to land loss and unequal treatment by the state. Set up in 1975, the Waitangi Tribunal has addressed breaches against Maori in the Treaty since its signing in 1840. The Waitangi Tribunal itself was the culmination of the long history of strained Maori-Pakeha relations, which, especially from the 1970s onwards, saw a return to Maori cultural roots and the emergence of Maori cultural nationalism, often in opposition to Pakeha. The term *biculturalism*, on the other hand, which first appeared during this time, emphasizes the political vision of New Zealand's two founding cultures living in harmony in one nation, or of one nation participating and sharing in both cultures. Yet, the politics of biculturalism continues to be contested. Critics of the term say that New Zealand should be a multicultural society, acknowledging the existence and rights of new immigrant communities instead of privileging only the two founding cultures. Others say that biculturalism is not at all fully realized, arguing for better representation of Maori in state institutions (Hayward 2012).

In contrast to a national narrative that seems primarily concerned with how the past affects the present and how cultural identities are formed with reference to an often fixed historical discourse, Hulme's fiction presents us with a vision of a protean world, abundant with a "perverse generativity," a term I borrow from Marina Warner (Warner 2002, 76). In *Fantastic Metamorphoses, Other Worlds: Ways of Telling the Self* (2002), Warner investigates a variety of approaches that question our received definitions of human identity and psychological development. Central to her argument is the notion that the processes of metamorphosis, mutation, and incubation offer new ways of thinking about the self, facilitated by Europe's encounter with the cultures and stories of its colonies.[3] Most radical among these concepts, and the most useful in reading Hulme, are insect metamorphosis and mythical stories of human-insect hybridity found in indigenous cultures. Insect gestation undermines "the prevailing teleological view of natural development" according to which "the future should be deducible from the seed and the outcome appropriate" (Warner 2002, 79). Insect metamorphosis, therefore, "introduces permutations of dissimilarity, not of similarity, into the development of an entity" (Warner 2002, 79). The caterpillar does not give us any clues as to what the butterfly will look like. Often brightly colored caterpillars develop into dull-looking moths and vice versa. The process of pupating in this context "produces something entirely unpredictable: the parent in this case does not ensure any recognizable feature of the offspring" (Warner 2002, 85). Insects appear throughout Hulme's fiction, sometimes literally and sometimes more symbolically, but always questioning notions of personal identity and tribal affiliation in the contexts of environmental debates and the shifting trends in bicultural relations in New Zealand. To further examine these ideas, my essay engages with two of Hulme's short stories in more detail: "Hooks and Feelers" from *Te Kaihau/The Windeater* and "Hatchings" from *Stonefish.*

"Hooks and Feelers" addresses many of the central themes of Hulme's *The Bone People* and can be read as continuous with the novel. Many of Hulme's characters are social outsiders, not fully part of either Maori or Pakeha communities. They are in liminal social positions, often of mixed race, asexual like Kerewin in *The Bone People*, or otherwise queer. In many cases, acts of extreme violence (physical, emotional, or both) further push these characters to the margins of their communities. While this experience isolates them from each other, Hulme's texts also imagine solutions that draw these lonely characters back together to form a new kind of community, or to create a new family structure that defies genetic kinship and traditional gender roles. Many of these issues have been explored in critical responses to *The Bone People.*[4] The triad of Kerewin, Joe, and Simon creates what has often been aligned with a utopian family unit that reinvents not only cultural but also sexual and gender identity: an adopted castaway child of ambiguous gender and uncertain genealogy, a bisexual half-Maori, half-Pakeha man who takes on the mothering role, and an asexual female artist who takes on the traditional paternal role by offering both Joe and Simon "that unlikely gift, her name" (Hulme 1985, 444).

The nameless family triad in "Hooks and Feelers" shares many similarities with the one in *The Bone People*. The mother is an artist who spends her days in her studio, absorbed in her work, while the father fulfills the maternal role, preparing dinner and looking after their son. Like the triad in *The Bone People*, the family in "Hooks and Feelers," consisting of a Maori mother, a Pakeha father, and a mixed-race child, represents New Zealand's bicultural society in nuclear form. In addition to the question of what makes us human, "Hooks and Feelers" also engages with the painful realization that all humans are mortal. The story further illustrates Hulme's use of Christian, especially Catholic, imagery. Told from the father's perspective and initially focussing on the son, who has prosthetic surgery after his hand is crushed in the door of the family car, the main themes of "Hooks and Feelers" are love, death, violence, and loss. As in *The Bone People*, violence is a barometer of strained Maori-Pakeha relations and as in *The Bone People*, violence becomes ambiguously tied to love. For this and related reasons, Otto Heim, reflecting on Susan Ash's essay "*The bone people* after *Te Kaihau*," regards *The Bone People* and *Te Kaihau/The Windeater* as "different articulations of the same vision" (Heim 1998, 123).

The boy's injury is caused by the mother who, angry with the boy for spilling a bag of peanuts all over the car, slams the car door shut without looking. Too damaged to be restored, the child's hand is surgically removed and replaced with a "permanent implant, with a special prosthesis that fits into it" (Hulme 1986, 84), the "hook" of the story title. The injury and subsequent replacement of the limb with a prosthesis leave the boy traumatized and emotionally remote, resulting in the father referring to him as "[m]y dear cool son" (Hulme 1986, 80). The prosthesis, attached to "an undamaged portion of sinew and nerve" (Hulme 1986, 84), together with the emotional coldness perceived by the father, make the boy appear less human—or as something other than human as Hulme might suggest, a bionic being, half child, half machine, who also begins to act in ways no longer entirely human. On his return from the hospital, the boy proceeds to destroy his favorite doll by throwing it in the fire, changing his mind at the last minute and snatching the half-singed head back out of the flames with his new unfeeling "hand," saying "On second thoughts, I'll keep this" (Hulme 1986, 78). Otto Heim argues that *Te Kaihau/The Windeater* presents us with characters "whose handicapped situation in some ways prepares them for unaccountable experiences" (Heim 1998, 195). For the boy in "Hooks and Feelers," the use of his hook presents him with an experience that has no precedent in his family or wider social circle. He has to negotiate this new reality on his own, and as a result he becomes, at least initially, emotionally withdrawn in a period of symbolic pupation or incubation. Later he will emerge as a new person with abilities for connection that reach far beyond those of any of his community.

The emotionally disturbed child, half Maori and half Pakeha, also acts as a metaphor for the disturbed bicultural relations in New Zealand. The representation and indeed the very presence of violence in New Zealand literature is indicative of how the country negotiates its postcolonial history, isolating both communities from each other. For Hulme, the political vision of biculturalism is a real possibility for New Zealand's future, even though it may remain unrealized in the political present and was only beginning to be articulated when she was writing the story. Like Simon in *The Bone People*, the child in "Hooks and Feelers" is also a catalyst for healing, and like Simon, he is equated with Christ. In both texts, the crucifix plays a central role and creates a direct link between the suffering of Christ and the suffering of the boys. The boy's artist mother in "Hooks and Feelers" has covered the crucifix in her studio with a black cloth, leaving only one hand exposed. The text describes the accident in a way that leaves no doubt as to the direct alignment of the boy's ordeal with Christ's crucifixion: "He was nailed, pinioned against the side of the car by his trapped hand" (Hulme 1986, 85).

At the beginning of the story, the day before the accident, we see the woman in the act of creating a series of "tall fluted goblets" on her potter's wheel for the whole family to "drink wine together" (Hulme 1986, 77), echoing a communion rite and, by extension, the Last Supper as well as the mysteries of the Holy Grail. Later these goblets are destroyed and become cones that seem to have no obvious purpose. The text is never explicit about what the cones are for but implies, in conjunction with the crucifix scene, that they are the artist's attempt to model a "hand" for the boy. The mother later destroys the cones and remolds them into wine cups she calls "[k]raters," to which the father responds "they should sell well" (Hulme 1986, 86). The text here points to the powerlessness of art in the face of human tragedy or rather, albeit in a cursory way, suggests that today's art as commodity has lost the numinous power to heal that it once had. Hulme does not pursue this idea further here, but the reader familiar with *The Bone People* is reminded of a similar issue affecting Kerewin, who after winning the lottery can buy everything her heart desires, including time for her art, but her creativity loses its power as a result of this.

The loss of the boy's hand initially and predictably creates a rift between mother and child that culminates in the boy inflicting a wound on the mother's left breast with his "hook" in a gesture that parallels the violence of the initial injury. This retributive act is a catalyst that restores the loving bond between mother and child. Once atonement has taken place, the focus of the text shifts to the mother. The tragedy of the second part of the story, particularly in the eyes of the narrator father, becomes the mother's death from cancer. In this sense, the loss of the boy's hand is a foreshadowing of the mother's loss of life. Continuing the many Christian references in the text, this family triad also evokes the holy family.[5] The mother's clay embodying an "idea" recalls the act of creation in Genesis (where man is made from clay and brought to life by divine breath) as well as the immaculate conception of the Virgin Mary (the spirit of god becoming incarnate in the "vessel" of Mary's womb). The mother's reluctance to fully communicate with her husband on the matter of the cones evokes the passage from the gospel of St. Luke: "But Mary kept all these things, and pondered them in her heart" (Luke 2:19). The mother's lack of communication leaves her a dark, shadowy mystery that the narrator compares to the great sea of Kiwa, "te moananui a Kiwa" (Hulme 1986, 82), the Maori name for the Pacific and the location of the mythical ancestral home Hawaiki. As an embodiment of the ocean, the mother is also other than human, more mythical sea creature than woman, "her black hair wreathed about her body like seaweed" (Hulme 1986, 82): ". . . I must keep on going down into her greeny deeps, down to where her face is, to where the soft anemone tentacles of her fingers beckon and sway and sweep me onward to the weeping heart of the world" (Hulme 1986, 82).

In the wider context of the holy family, the father, like Joseph, questions his paternity: "How can he be my son and have so little of me in him?"— adding: "But his strange cold nature comes from neither of us" (83), suggesting that the boy is somehow altogether "other," either through his connection to the hook/machine or because he is god incarnate. Linked to this otherness is Hulme's image of the shining cuckoo, "a summer migrant to New Zealand" (*New Zealand Birds Online* 2013). Heim and Zimmermann argue that the story "Nightsong for the Shining Cuckoo," also collected in *Te Kaihau/ The Windeater*, creates the image of a cuckoo child, with the shining cuckoo combining the notion of uprooting and loss of tradition with the symbolic meaning of spring and the return of new life (Heim and Zimmermann 1992, 120). The child in "Hooks and Feelers" can be seen as a cuckoo child not only because of his otherness but also because the ideas of loss and rebirth connect in his person.[6]

The new evolving bond between mother and son is emphasized by the boy's singing a line from the Corpus Christi Carol, with reference to another bird—"the falcon hath borne my make away" (Hulme 1986, 89)—which suggests that the boy knows of the mother's imminent death.[7] The Corpus Christi Carol is a Middle English hymn often associated with the Grail legend, in particular the maimed king or Fisher King.[8] In Shirley Stave's reading of the holy family in *The Bone People*, Simon's brutal beating at the center of the novel is compared to Christ's crucifixion. The joining of all three protagonists in a new family unit at the end of the novel becomes possible only after "Simon's crucifixion and resurrection" (Stave 2011, 29).

Simon and the child in "Hooks and Feelers" are thus aligned both with the dying and risen Christ as well as the Fisher King of the Corpus Christi Carol. The newly established bond between mother and son in "Hooks and Feelers," of which the reference to the Corpus Christi Carol is a symbolic expression, can also be read as a post-crucifixion and resurrection development. In this scene, the other half of the story's title comes into play: the hook causes pain, but the song, and the emotion it expresses, creates "feelers" that reach out and connect. The boy's un-childlike knowing of the mother's impending death emphasizes the notion of a supernatural connection, suggesting that between Mary and Christ, with the father feeling like the merely human Joseph.

In linking spirituality and technology, science and faith, Hulme's story transcends the postcolonial rifts between the communities of contemporary New Zealand as well as conventional religious discourses. The child becomes a signifier of radical difference. Hulme's representation of difference in this case evokes the philosophy of Emmanuel Levinas, whose concept of alterity raises epistemic, ontological, as well as ethical questions. In *Totality and Infinity* (1961), Levinas argues: "Western philosophy has most often been an ontology: a reduction of the other to the same . . ." (Levinas 1969, 43). Levinas proposes a different kind of alterity, one that manifests not in a negation of the self, but "καθ'αύτό," by and of itself (Levinas 1969, 51). The Other retains "his irreducibility to the I" (Levinas 1969, 43); it cannot be translated into what is familiar to the self, and as such it demands an engagement on its own terms, which, for Levinas, translates into an ethics. In other words, the Other "can be neither comprehended nor refused" (Kearney 2003, 71). Hulme's boy appears to be a misfit only when read *in relation to* or *as a negation of* the family and wider community around him (i.e., only by conventional human or cultural standards). Hulme, on the other hand, invites us to engage with the boy's otherness as something that "resists possession, resists my powers" (Levinas 1969, 197) and, instead, requires "infinite responsibility" (Kearney 2003, 67).

By touching on issues of radical difference, "Hooks and Feelers" questions traditional family units and kinship patterns, the latter particularly important in Maori culture. In this context, the "feelers" of the title also evoke the organs with which insects acquire knowledge about their surroundings, suggesting that the child has indeed undergone a period of pupation and transformation that has now prepared him "for unaccountable experiences" (Heim 1998, 195). As such, the feelers as organs connect the individual to the wider world and help ascertain the individual's place within it. They help overcome the habitual isolation that characterizes many of Hulme's protagonists, including the family in this story.[9] In addition, the implications of insect metamorphosis set out at the beginning of this essay come into play here as insect gestation "introduces permutations of dissimilarity, not of similarity, into the development of an entity" (Warner 2002, 79). In the context of "Hooks and Feelers," it is a very clear indication that "the parent in this case does not ensure any recognizable feature of the off-spring" (Warner 2002, 85). This aspect of dissimilarity contains the seed of Hulme's utopian revision of New Zealand's bicultural life towards a truly integrated and connected rather than divided society, a society where each component can be "other" καθ'αύτό and still contribute meaningful-ly to a common social vision.

Heim points out that Hulme's work is often classed as distinctly postmod-ern, arguing that it "articulates a discursive conflict, a certain refusal to be fully identified with the discourses one must use. As such it indeed serves to express a specific Maoriness, albeit one that seriously questions any received notion of cultural authenticity" (Heim 1998, 106). Echoing the notion ex-pressed in "feelers," Mark Williams observes: "Hulme's favourite image in *the bone people* of interwoven threads is a useful one. It implies that cultural traditions can be allowed their discrete integrity, yet worked together into new patterns. It is also noteworthy that she seeks to include a variety of traditions, including European ones, in that reworking" (Williams 1990, 109). In this context, "Hooks and Feelers" works as a critique of Maori cultural nationalism. Hulme's non-traditional engagement with social institu-tions as well as issues largely interpreted in conservative terms in both Maori and Pakeha communities alike attempts to critique the divisive legacies of biculturalism as it envisions new social models. "Hooks and Feelers" there-fore symbolically enacts the ideas expressed in insect metamorphosis: the creation and embrace of difference as personal and social vision.

In *Te Kaihau/The Windeater*, the social and cultural divisions inherent in biculturalism are mirrored in an often hostile environment. In many of the texts, the land has a sinister "personality," as in "A Tally of the Souls of Sheep," or the way humans interact with the environment is reflective of social interaction, as in "The Cicadas of Summer." In "A Tally," the coastal land and its inhabitants conspire to kidnap two children; the land may literal-ly have swallowed them, or one of its "natives" has committed an act of cannibalism as the last line of the story seems to imply, whereas in "The Cicadas of Summer" the girl's "consumption of the cicada nymphs foreshad-ows the consumption of the girl," that is, her rape and murder (Seran 2013, 2). *Stonefish* continues to foreground environmental factors. However, in *Stonefish* Hulme's interrogation of the ecological impact of contemporary civilization on human culture assumes a more pronounced engagement with the possibility of radical difference in a biological and environmental sense. The collection also speaks directly to aspects of pupating and the symbolic meanings this part of insect metamorphosis has for Hulme's utopian vision. "Hatchings" engages with this theme quite literally.

Told from the perspective of an elderly woman, whose lifelong passion has been observing the life cycle of the gum emperor-moth on the family gum tree plantation, "Hatchings" reflects on ideas of family, community, and the long after-effects of New Zealand's colonization by Europe. The text sketches the story of a family, part or wholly Maori (the story is not explicit about this), who has made a living as gum tree planters. Gum trees have been imported into New Zealand from Australia since the beginning of New Zealand's colonization by European settlers to remedy the deforestation of the islands and introduce rot-resistant timber for construction work (Judd and Menefy 2002). Gum emperor-moths also came from Australia, probably as pupa on imported wood or blowing in from the Tasman Sea (*Farm Forestry New Zealand* 2009; White 1972, 669). Insect infestation has affected the gum tree industry in New Zealand considerably (Judd and Menefy 2002; White 1972, 672), a fact that is at the heart of Hulme's story. But the story also reflects on the wider issues of colonization. Gum trees or eucalypts have been circulated globally for centuries, and today "eucalypts are the most widely planted hardwood trees in the world" (Judd and Menefy 2002). In some places, "such as California and South Africa, eucalypts have become so entrenched as both amenity and forestry trees it is hard to believe they are not natives" (Judd and Menefy 2002). Yet, as a foreign plant eucalyptus has not always been welcome because its presence has changed native landscapes considerably.

Focusing on a particular insect and its habitat, "Hatchings" engages with colonization at the level of botanic and animal migration and takes as its starting point the ecological impact of transplantation in the global circuit of empire and the capitalist economy. In the course of the story, however, the notion of hatching touches on the various metaphorical, social, and mythical meanings of moths and their life cycles, both in a Western and Maori context. Like "Hooks and Feelers," "Hatchings" is a story about life and death, love and the loss of love, and the pain and isolation that accompanies familial estrangement. Jim, the protagonist's husband, has a violent temper that isolates him increasingly from his family and eventually confines him to a mental institution. The story intimates that Jim's rage is the result of his time as a soldier in World War II, presumably untreated and undiagnosed PTSD, which only fully unfolds over time. The story suggests that Jim has been incubating this rage in a similar way to the pupating moths observed by his wife that incubate their true self. First Jim's rage manifests in his aversion to sex, then his indignation about the gum moths' attack of his plantations, and in his burning his wife's moth diaries, driving him further and further into isolation. Eventually, his full rage bursts out and he burns down the house, ruins the plantation, and attacks his wife with a slasher. This gradual unfolding of rage mimics the gradual process of insect pupation.

Another story of rage and violence in the family line is also told in images suggesting pupation. The elderly protagonist's Maori great-grandfather, referred to as Pōua, was imprisoned for three weeks in a whale-oil cask by Pakeha whalers as punishment for not alerting them to an approaching *taua*.[10] The humiliating experience of being locked up in the cask, "cramped, stinking, hungry, thirst quenched with a tin mug of water twice a day" (Hulme 2004, 130), changes Pōua completely. He emerges from the cask, his metaphorical pupa, a different man, and his appearance resembles that of the emperor-moth: "Pōua's hair had turned white but his eyes were huge and glowed" (Hulme 2004, 130). The fully grown gum emperor-moth has a furry covering around the body that is partly white and eyes that are large compared with its size. Pōua has also acquired psychic gifts he did not have before: ". . . afterwards, Pōua could call his people without opening his mouth. He could tell when any of us were going to die. He knew to the day how long he would live" (Hulme 2004, 130). In other words, Pōua has died to his old self and has been reborn, another implication of the pupa stage, making him open to "unaccountable experiences."

It is only through the story of Pōua that the reader knows of the family's Maori ancestry. The English names of the other family members suggest that they have lost their link to their Maori heritage and assumed English names, as many Maori did over the past century, owing to urbanization and resulting in communities becoming fragmented (Moura-Koçoglu 2009, 34). Another possibility is that the family has intermarried with Pakeha since the incident involving Pōua. Either way, the implication is of a loss of roots mirrored in the protagonist's fractured family. Yet, the moth imagery that pervades the story points a way out of cultural fragmentation and individual isolation. In terms of conservationist environmentalism, the introduction of foreign plant and animal life like that of the gum tree and its moth may involve a potential threat to any ecosystem, especially the fragile island environments of the Pacific, but in this story it becomes the saving element. The protagonist's meticulous observation of the emperor-moths' life cycle reveals subtle mutations over time that help the moths adapt and survive in a new environment: "Moths that had always been shades of brown—sepia, dun, tawny—have begun to develop greenish sheens. Our eucalypts stay mainly green in the hottest summer . . ." (Hulme 2004, 123). The protagonist also notes the effects of poisons on the environment, creating "monsters" as she calls them, maimed moths unable to walk or fly. But she also observes naturally occurring "strangeness" or "ambiguity" (Hulme 2004, 129), moths that occasionally have the physical characteristics of both the male and female of the species and "lack entirely a male's interest in females" (Hulme 2004, 129). These she compares to her son Carlin who, the story infers, is either gay or transgender, who has settled down with his beloved and seems to be the only family member who lives a happy and fulfilled life. In this way, "Hatchings" continues Hulme's idea of indeterminate gender identities and non-traditional families as a way to imagine healing the rifts in contemporary New Zealand society, here characterized again by divisive violence and rage. Carlin and the queer moths are thus another form of the cuckoo or wild child.

The end of the story intimates that the protagonist is about to die. Observing the moths hatching on her windowsill one by one, there is one cocoon that still has not hatched. She can hear scratching inside, so the hatching is imminent, as she falls asleep. The story intimates that the protagonist slips into death, and the pupa ready to hatch is symbolic of her soul being released from the cocoon of her body. As such, the story plays on Western symbols of the soul that in classical traditions is often depicted as a butterfly (the Greek for "psyche" translates as both soul and butterfly). However, moths have a similar meaning in Maori mythology, where they represent the souls of the dead (Best 2016, 71). By mixing the two traditions in one image, Hulme creates a composite metaphor that imaginatively bridges the divide between Maori and Pakeha. The protagonist's death also makes room for a new generation of New Zealanders, who may be better equipped to negotiate the lingering challenges of biculturalism. The end of the story suggests that Carlin and others similar to him—people of mixed race who embrace difference, indeterminacy, and liminality—are the true heirs of New Zealand's biculturalism. The protagonist knows that Carlin will keep the family gum tree plantation "as a sanctuary for as long as he lives" (Hulme 2004, 133), thus honoring the work of his parents.

The house of the nation, Hulme's story suggests, built by many generations of New Zealanders, Maori and Pakeha alike, will and should be cherished by the generations of the future. At the same time, how one lives in it will have to change. Heim and Zimmermann observe that in her early essay, "Mauri: An Introduction to Bi-cultural Poetry in New Zealand," Hulme is very clear about the position of mixed-race communities and their potential to contribute to a true vision of biculturalism: "While she stresses that the experience of being of dual ancestry can be painful and heart-rending, she maintains that 'Maori poetry written in English . . . is the most vital, stimulating, and innovative force in New Zealand writing today'" (Heim and Zimmermann 1992, 110; Hulme 1981, 295). For Hulme, writers of mixed race are "of double beginning, inhabiting both *Te Ao Maori* and *Te Ao Pakeha*, but writing for *Te Ao Hou*" (Hulme 1981, 296, in Heim and Zimmermann 1992, 110). One could argue that the nameless mixed-race child in "Hooks and Feelers" remains nameless because this "double beginning" had no place, and thus no name, yet in the New Zealand of the 1970s and 1980s when the stories of *Te Kaihau/The Windeater* were written.[11] Likewise, Carlin and the moth mutations aligned with him in "Hatchings" are only tentatively named, indicating that even at the later time of *Stonefish*, writing and living for *Te Ao Hou* was and may still be today a long way away from being embraced by all.

*Te Kaihau/The Windeater* and *Stonefish* address ecocritical debates by interrogating the "interconnections between nature and culture" and by attempting "a theoretical discourse [that] negotiates between the human and the non-human" (Glotfelty 1996, xix). Ecocritical interventions in postcolonial literature, such as those by Graham Huggan, have argued that while it may appear as though postcolonial writing has been solely concerned with the sociological and historical implications of colonization, "postcolonial criticism has effectively renewed, rather than belatedly discovered, its commitment to the environment" (Huggan 2004, 702). Huggan argues that postcolonial literature actually insists "on the inseparability of current crises of ecological mismanagement from historical legacies of imperialistic exploitation and authoritarian abuse" (Huggan 2004, 702). While ecocritical debates in postcolonial contexts have themselves become more diverse since Huggan's publication,[12] Hulme's work engages with this connection between ecological mismanagement and imperialist exploitation that Huggan first observed. In *Stonefish,* mutant life forms are the environment's reaction to pollution and climate change, acting as visible reminders of an exploitation that goes beyond the human-centered debates on postcolonial hybridity and New Zealand's bicultural relations. Hulme's is essentially a biocentric outlook. Her writing expresses an understanding that all life forms are connected, an understanding that reflects her Maori roots.[13] Most importantly, her work demonstrates how the exploitation of and disrespect towards the planet's resources act as a mirror and barometer of the way we conduct our interpersonal and intercultural relationships.

## NOTES

1. Bachs are holiday beach cabins, an iconic part of New Zealand's coastal landscapes and cultural life. Cribs is the term more widely used on South Island.

2. A major and groundbreaking anthology of postcolonial science fiction, *So Long Been Dreaming*, was published in 2004. Though the publication of science fiction texts by postcolonial writers or on postcolonial themes predates this anthology, scholarship in the field—and the conceptualization of the term—has come into its own largely after this date.

3. Warner uses Europe's encounter with the Americas as her starting point, but the concepts she develops are applicable in a number of contexts involving cultural contact zones.

4. See, for example, Anna Smith, 1995, "Keri Hulme and 'Love's Wounded Beings,'" or Otto Heim, 1998, *Writing Along Broken Lines*, on the wider context of violence in New Zealand literature.

5. For a related reading of the holy family in *The Bone People* see Stave. Stave argues that as the birth and teachings of Jesus "heralded the way for a fusion of Jew and Gentile," so Hulme's holy family in *The Bone People* points towards a new social order in which the different strands of New Zealand society are integrated (Stave 2011, 26). The holy family in Hulme's short fiction has the same function and meaning.

6. The cuckoo child also appears as the trope of the "wild child" in New Zealand writing and has a similar function in this context: "In West Coast fiction these elements combine in the

figure of the 'wild child,' often intellectually or emotionally challenged and/or challenging, independent of conventional family structures and acting as a catalyst for adult interactions, which has emerged as a major theme in the literature" (Dawber 2012, 3).

7. Melvin E. Bradford reads the falcon in the refrain of the Corpus Christi Carol as the "falcon of death," separating two lovers who are also imagined as birds (Bradford 1970, 169).

8. This is the full text of the Corpus Christi Carol:

> *Lulley, lully, lulley, lully,*
> *The faucon hath born my mak away.*
> He bare hym up, he bare hym down,
> He bare hym into an orchard brown.
> In that orchard ther was an hall,
> That was hanged with purpill and pall.
> And in that hall ther was a bede,
> Hit was hangid with gold so rede.
> And yn that bed ther lythe a knyght,
> His wowndes bledyng day and nyght.
> By that bedes side ther kneleth a may,
> And she wepeth both nyght and day.
> And by that bedes side ther stondith a ston,
> "Corpus Christi" wretyn theron

9. Ann-Mari Hedbäck engages with the meanings of "hooks" and "feelers" slightly differently, but she is equally attuned to the contradictory meanings contained in each. In relation to "feelers," she argues that "there is no substitute for the gentle touch of the fingers, for feelers" while her reading of "hooks" include "hooks in the heart," an understanding of the various layers of pain invoked by loss in the story (Hedbäck 1996, 147). In relation to the latter, she even goes as far as to infer that the father could have killed his sick wife (Hedbäck 1996, 147), though her reading provides no persuasive evidence for this suggestion.

10. A taua is a Maori war party, a traditional form of warfare.

11. At the very end of the story, the narrative suggests that the boy's given name may have been Charleston, after the modelling clay used by the mother for her pottery, but this gestures more towards the symbolic meaning of Mary modelling Christ in her womb (the mother's pregnancy is obliquely referenced in this passage) than an actual name.

12. See, for example, the essays collected in DeLoughrey and Handley, eds., 2011, *Postcolonial Ecologies*, and DeLoughrey, Didur, and Carrigan, eds., 2015, *Global Ecologies and the Environmental Humanities*.

13. See Hulme's essays in *Homeplaces*, stories such as "Getting It" in *Stonefish*, as well as Te Ahukaramū Charles Royal, 2005, "First peoples in Māori tradition—Ancestors from the natural world." Of related interest may be Ann-Catherine Nabholz, 1998, "Animals in Keri Hulme's *Te Kaihau/The Windeater*: Reflections on Biocentric Egalitarianism." See also DeLoughrey, 2015, for an in-depth reading of these debates in *Stonefish*.

# BIBLIOGRAPHY

Ash, Susan. 1989. "*The bone people* after *Te Kaihau*." *World Literatures Written in English* 29.1: 123–35.

Best, Elsdon. 2016. "Maori Religion and Mythology Part 2: The Spirit World." *New Zealand Electronic Text Collection/Te Pūhikotui o Aotearoa*. Accessed December 19, 2018. http://nzetc.victoria.ac.nz/tm/scholarly/tei-Bes02Reli-t1-body-d2-d5.html.

Bradford, Melvin E. 1970. "Come Slowly All Together: A Reading of the 'Corpus Christi Carol.'" *The South Central Bulletin* 30.4: 168–71.

Dawber, Carol. 2012. "Voices of the West Coast: An Investigation into the Development of a Distinctive West Coast Character in New Zealand Fiction." PhD diss. University of Canterbury.

DeLoughrey, Elizabeth, and George B. Handley, eds. 2011. *Postcolonial Ecologies: Literatures of the Environment.* Oxford: Oxford University Press.

DeLoughrey, Elizabeth. 2015. "Ordinary Futures: Interspecies Worlding in the Anthropocene." In *Global Ecologies and the Environmental Humanities: Postcolonial Approaches*, 352–72, edited by Elizabeth DeLoughrey, Jill Didur, and Anthony Carrigan. New York/London: Routledge.

Farm Forestry New Zealand. 2009. "Gum Emperor-moth." *Forest and Timber Insects in New Zealand* No. 7. Based on P. J. Alma (1977). Accessed December 19, 2018. http://www.nzffa.org.nz/farm-forestry-model/the-essentials/forest-health-pests-and-diseases/Pests/Antheraea-eucalypti/Gum-emperor-mothEnt07.

Glotfelty, Cheryll. 1996. "Introduction: Literary Studies in an Age of Environmental Crisis." In *The Ecocriticism Reader: Landmarks in Literary Ecology*, xv–xxxvii, edited by Cheryll Glotfelty and Harold Fromm. Athens: University of Georgia Press.

Hall, Sandie. 1984. "Conversation at Okarito; Sandie Hall and Keri Hulme talk about *The Bone People*." *Broadsheet* 121 (1984): 16–21.

Hayward, Janine. 2012. "Biculturalism." *Te Ara—the Encyclopedia of New Zealand.* Accessed December 19, 2018. https://teara.govt.nz/en/biculturalism.

Hedbäck, Ann-Mari. 1996. "Keri Hulme: Scriptwriter and Storyteller." In *Defining New Idioms and Alternative Forms of Expression*, 145–52, edited by Eckhart Breitinger. ASNEL Papers 1. Amsterdam/Atlanta: Rodopi.

Heim, Otto. 1998. *Writing Along Broken Lines: Violence and Ethnicity in Contemporary Maori Fiction.* Auckland: Auckland University Press.

Heim, Otto, and Anna Zimmermann. 1992. "Hu(l)man Medi(t)ations: Inter-Cultural Explorations in Keri Hulme's The Windeater/Te Kaihau." *Australian and New Zealand Studies in Canada* 8: 106–35.

Hopkinson, Nalo and Uppinder Mehan, eds. 2004. *So Long Been Dreaming: Postcolonial Science Fiction and Fantasy.* Vancouver: Arsenal Pulp Press.

Huggan, Graham. 2004. "'Greening' Postcolonialism: Ecocritical Perspectives." *Modern Fiction Studies* 50.3: 701–33.

Hulme, Keri. 1981. "Mauri: An Introduction to Bi-Cultural Poetry in New Zealand." In *Only Connect: Literary Perspectives East and West*, 290–310, edited by Guy Amirthanayagam and Syd C. Harrex. Adelaide: Centre for Research in the New Literatures in English; Honolulu: East-West Center.

————. 1985. *The Bone People.* Auckland/London: Spiral in association with Hodder and Stoughton.

————. 1986. *Te Kaihau/The Windeater.* Wellington: Victoria University Press.

————. 1989. *Homeplaces: Three Coasts of the South Island of New Zealand.* Photographs by Robin Morrison. Auckland: Hodder & Stoughton.

————. 2004. *Stonefish.* Wellington: Huia.

Judd, Warren and Diana Menefy. 2002. "Eucalypts: Trees of the Future?" *New Zealand Geographic* 058. Accessed December 19, 2018. https://www.nzgeo.com/stories/eucalypts-trees-of-the-future/.

Kearney, Richard. 2003. *Strangers, Gods and Monsters: Interpreting Otherness.* London/New York: Routledge.

Keenan, Danny. 2017. "New Zealand Wars—New Zealand Wars Overview." *Te Ara—The Encyclopedia of New Zealand.* Accessed December 19, 2018. https://teara.govt.nz/en/new-zealand-wars/page-1.

Keown, Michelle. 2007. *Pacific Islands Writing: The Postcolonial Literatures of Aotearoa/New Zealand and Oceania.* Oxford: Oxford University Press.

Levinas, Emmanuel. (1961) 1969. *Totality and Infinity: An Essay in Exteriority.* Translated by Alphonso Lingis. Pittsburgh: Duquesne University Press.

Moura-Koçoglu, Michaela. 2009. "Swarming with Ghosts and Turehus: Indigenous Language and Concepts in Contemporary Maori Writing." In *Translation of Cultures*, 133–47, edited by Petra Rüdiger and Konrad Gross. Amsterdam: Rodopi.

Nabholz, Ann-Catherine. 1998. "Animals in Keri Hulme's *Te Kaihau/The Windeater*: Reflections on Biocentric Egalitarianism." *Commonwealth Essay and Studies* 20.2: 40–53.

*New Zealand Birds Online: The Digital Encyclopaedia of New Zealand Birds*. 2013. "Shining Cuckoo." Accessed December 19, 2018. http://nzbirdsonline.org.nz/species/shining-cuckoo.

*New Zealand History/Nga korero a ipurangi o Aotearoa* (*Ministry for Culture and Heritage*). 2014. "The Treaty in Practice—Slide to War." Accessed December 19, 2018. https://nzhistory.govt.nz/politics/treaty/the-treaty-in-practice/slide-to-war.

Royal, Te Ahukaramū Charles. 2005. "First peoples in Māori tradition—Ancestors from the natural world." *Te Ara—the Encyclopedia of New Zealand*. Accessed December 19, 2018. https://teara.govt.nz/en/first-peoples-in-maori-tradition/page-4.

Seran, Justine. 2013. "Tales of Torment: Death, Nature, and Genre in Keri Hulme's Short Story Collection *Te Kaihau/The Windeater*." *FORUM: University of Edinburgh Postgraduate Journal of Culture and the Arts* 16: 1–13. Accessed December 19, 2018. http://www.forumjournal.org/article/view/523/811.

Smith, Anna. 1995. "Keri Hulme and 'Love's Wounded Beings.'" In *Opening the Book: New Essays on New Zealand Writing*, 140–61, edited by Michelle Leggott and Mark Williams. Auckland: Auckland University Press.

Stave, Shirley A. 2011. "Keri Hulme's Holy Family: Postcoloniality and Theology in *The Bone People*." *Journal of Commonwealth and Postcolonial Studies* 17.1: 20–39.

Warner, Marina. 2002. *Fantastic Metamorphoses, Other Worlds: Ways of Telling the Self*. Oxford: Oxford University Press.

White, T. C. R. 1972. "The Distribution, Dispersal and Host Range of Antheraea Eucalypti (Lepidoptera: Saturniidae) in New Zealand." *Pacific Insects* 14.4: 669–73. Accessed December 19, 2018. http://hbs.bishopmuseum.org/pi/pdf/14(4)-669.pdf.

Williams, Mark. 1990. *Leaving the Highway: Six Contemporary New Zealand Novelists*. Auckland: Auckland University Press.

## Chapter Five

# Magical Realism

*Narrative Play and Historical Jokes*

Stéphanie Walsh Matthews

Magical realism, a literary genre or mode, provokes a clash between oppositional systems that may, at times, inherently beckon the grotesque.[1] As magic realism's narrative is weaved and tangled through a myriad of voices, characters, timelines, and optics, the effect of combining seamlessly the real and the supernatural allows for not only an inter-textual cornucopia, but for a textual space that provides optimum room for subversive discourses. The grotesque, which can be characterized by the oppositional push and pull of attraction and repulsion, suits magic realism, as the clash at the narrative level resonates with the various shocks and dissonances that are vested at the thematic core of the magical real novel. Beyond the weird of the magical real, there is a locatable element, a source, one that provokes reaction— much like the grotesque—that is, instead, rather endearing. It's something known as "humor."

Magical realism's chief characteristic is the interplay of real and magical events. To this primary attribute, a long list of possible elements, including the use of irony or parody, postcolonial ideas and frames, or textual subversive mechanics, are tacked on to help in labeling a work as magical real. However, as I have theorized, it is the paradoxical co-habitation of magic and real elements (referred to as codes) that allows us to discuss magical real as a literary genre. Of course, other essential narrative qualities can include a *matter-of-fact* narrative voice and the mimetic invocation of historical events. Importantly, these same characteristics often warrant the association of magical realism with postcolonialism along with, of course, the context from which the text emerges.[2] For this matter, it is the play with the mimetic, which creates the parodied and ironic stances towards historical events, that evokes the liminal relationship between postcolonialism and magic realism, especially when considering the literature cited as magical real emanating from outside of Europe.

I would like to demonstrate how the juncture of codes of the magical and the real mimic the polarizing effects found in humor and, afterwards, how humor too is a subversive tool of magical realism. Humor, as we will discover, does not always necessarily subvert what we think it should.

## MAGIC REALISM[3]: A QUICK OVERVIEW

Magical realism is a genre (if we respect the original definition of genre as proposed by Tzetvan Todorov) or a mode (if we choose to accept Amaryll Chanady's more recent term)[4] that indiscriminately blends together magical and real events. It is the absence of comments from the narrator and characters that allows for the effect of "blurriness" or ineffability that appropriately describes the wonders of the stylized world that seems to resemble ours with, nonetheless, remarkable differences. It is this exact point that separates magic realism from the fantastic and fantasy. In other words, when reading a magical real text, one should be hard-pressed to determine what is real and what is not. Further complicating this blurry context is the use of historical events that help ground the mimetic plane. However, these same events are usurped and suddenly are transformed with impossible causes or consequences, changes are made to their trajectory, and their outcomes are reinvented. The multiple possibilities presented in the magical real novel allows for a repositioning of historical events. Because of this, theorists have assumed that the topsy-turvy nature of this modern novel's carnivalesque approach encourages a general reconceptualizing of the world. And because of these qualities, critics of the magical real novel have applied Bakhtin's theories on the dialogic to better understand the power of magical realism in contemporary terms. Moreover, because of the political and historical implications, coupled with the fact that the Latin American boom gave birth to one of the twentieth century's preferred genres, the postcolonial label was also quickly attached. Decentralization and disorientation of historical facts, accompanied by the narrative play with time and space, have also rendered magical realism an immediate bedfellow to postcolonialism.

In his work *Mimesis, Genres, and Postcolonial Discourse*, Stephen Slemon defines magic realism as postcolonial because magical real texts give a voice to the voiceless, place at the center those who have been marginalized, and create new codes capable of revealing something about the denied state or hidden reality that is liberating while also transmuting colonial violence. For these reasons, for the most part, until very recently, much of the critical work on magical realism inevitably entailed a postcolonial discourse as well (Slemon 1995, 146).

## Unfaithful Lovers

Because it was in Latin America that magic realism really boomed, it became heavily connected with that geographical space, as well as its political and social climate. As noted by Slemon:

> The term "magic realism" applies best to Garcia Marquez, who combines social concern and a free use of language. According to our more restrictive definition of the term, the magic realist aims at a basis of mimetic illusion while destroying it regularly with a strange treatment of time, space, characters, or what many people (in the Western world at least) take as the basic rules of the physical world. Magic realists usually have a definite idea of their social role and pose political problems, which beset the post-colonial country described. (Slemon 1995, 146)

Since the Latin American *boom*, magic realism has been located in other parts of the world. Along with Garcia Marquez's astonishing *One Hundred Years of Solitude* (1967), Salman Rushdie's *Midnight's Children* (1981) and Ben Okri's *Famished Road* (1991) also mark the epitome of the successful genre. Naturally, Patrick Suskind's *Grenouille* (1985) and Gunter Grass's *The Tin Drum* (1959) could equally slide into this category, but because of their European inheritance perhaps don't fit the mold here. Undeniably magical real novels by Rushdie, Marquez, and Okri play with notions of the imperial past, overthrow the assumptions of the contemporary, and mess around with space and time. The mimesis created, by and through the narrative, sketches a world paralleling the extra-textual universe by incorporating historical events and characters. This is done so that, as Kum Kum Sangari writes, magic realism "answers an emergent society's need for renewed self-description, and radical assessment, [displacing] the established categories through which the West had construed other cultures either in its own image or as alterity, [questioning] the western capitalist myth of modernization and progress, and [asserting] without nostalgia an indigenous preindustrial realm of possibility" (Sangari 1987, 162).

The natural lineage shared between magical realism and postcolonialism resides, then, primarily in social-political subversiveness. Subversity is offered up through altering portrayals of the past, as well as other reversals usually playing on accepted beliefs, be they mythological or religious, as well as on other cultural elements, such as gender and archetypal characters. History, however, serves as the greatest destabilizer, as it is, paradoxically, also the pillar of fact creating the mimesis in the magical real novel. It is for this reason that the treatment of history is of importance in this genre.

Playing with established historical truths evokes laughter, as Evelyn Fish-burn points out in her article "Humour and Magical Realism": "The comic always participates in the category of contradiction."[5] Fishburn discusses oppositional duality as being the mainspring for both magical realism and its underlying humor. She explains that humor in magical realism results from "the clash or collision when two contrasting or habitually incompatible asso-ciative contexts meet" (Fishburn 2005, 155). She adds that irony and parody also ensue from the coupling of the dissimilar and can provide ample deri-sion. Derision, I should add, is one of the many facets of subversion. As magic realism is characterized, primarily, by the oppositional co-existence of two codes, humor is thus a natural fit to its disjunction, much as the gro-tesque is, as pointed out earlier.

So it is then the association of disparate elements that is responsible for many of the unique qualities of magic realism. That being stated, the next question presents itself: If these texts are to be derisive and, by way of their postcolonial mandate, question authority, wouldn't laughter and other silly elements take away from the gravity of the content? To this, Fishburn argues that by decentering the dominant discourse, via laughter, cultural tensions are broken. Taboos can thus be entertained and shed some hopefully enlightened light on them. This subversive play dispels much of the dominant master-voice and brings out of the shadows the pre-colonial cultural elements for-gotten through imperial supremacy. That being said, we should be satisfied with the jester-like qualities of magical realism as it appears in the literatures of the colonized world. End of discussion. Right?

However, there is just one little problem. . . . There are texts that have been qualified as magical real that don't naturally fall into a postcolonial context but which, however, tend to play with history in the very same way. What do we do with those, I might ask? We should find it difficult to correct-ly attribute the postcolonial label to a large portion of magical realist litera-ture coming out of Canada and the US. Most importantly, as we will see, in the case of magical realism in Québécois literature, this label may even get us into some hot water! However, playing and joking with history is *de rigueur* in this highly engaging magical real corpus.

## Laughter in Non-Prescribed Postcolonial Magical Real Text

Much of the work done on magical realism tends to demonstrate "that magi-cal realism provides a means for writers to express a non-dominant or non-western perspective, whether that be from a feminist, postcolonial or rural standpoint, in opposition to dominant cultural discourse" (Bowers 2004, 102). This definition helps us out of the postcolonial bind we earlier found ourselves in. However, it does still imply that magical realism intrinsically creates derision, laughter, and criticism from the need to overturn dominant discourses (which is a rather postcolonial process). What if, instead, we could argue that through jokes and play, especially of a historical kind, particularities of the genre, far beyond simple rhetorical devices, can be underlined? Their postcolonial attributes would reside, then, not in the experience of reading, but in the text's analysis.

In order to illustrate the power of play and historical jokes, I will quickly demonstrate how Marquez's *One Hundred Years of Solitude* serves as a road map for the Québécois magical real novel *La Tribu* (*The Tribe*) by Québécois François Barcelo. Will Marquez's postcolonial discourses transpire in Barcelo's *The Tribe*? Will we still find texts like these funny?

## Demonstration

The invitation to compare these two texts comes from François Barcelo's dedication to Marquez at the start of his novel. In fact, *The Tribe* serves as a Québécois palimpsest to Marquez's *One Hundred Years.* However, intentionally, *The Tribe* plays on Marquez's novel. Is this autoreferentiality at its best? The elements of laughter and play in the story of Macondo are amplified and exaggerated in *The Tribe.* Four striking features are worth noting. The first is the level of amplification; the second, the playful use of real historical and temporal markers; the third, the role of the writer; and, finally, doubles and multiples of characters.

## Amplification

Marquez's epic novel offers irony and tragedy, intercepted by many comic elements. It recounts the story over one hundred years in the fictitious off-the-path village of Macondo. As if to up the ante, Barcelo's *The Tribe* is SUPER epic and extends beyond 25,000 years. *The Tribe* tells the story of one of Canada's supposed first tribes, led by the chief "Big Nose" who, most unfortunately, can't die.

Where Marquez exposes a number of real cataclysmic events in Colombia (such as the civil war, the war of independence, treaties, the strike of over 32,000 workers at the United Fruit Company of Boston, and the great massacre of Cienaga on December 5, 1928), Barcelo, in a similar fashion, retells the entire story of Québec, starting with a sixteenth-century meeting of a boy named Jean-François and the original 25,000 BC tribe of antler hunters. For that matter, Barcelo covers thousands of years: the Ice Age, Upper and Lower Canadian rifts, internment camps, Joan of Arc, Charlemagne, Adam and Eve, the American Civil War, Quebec's referendum, and the list goes on and on. Québécois postcolonial and magical real critic Marie Vautier rightly notes that Barcelo is playing with the temporal organization of history to destabilize the recognizable mimetic elements. However, when comparing

*The Tribe* to its mentor's mere *One Hundred Years*, on whom does this joke really seem to fall?

## Playing with Realist Anchors

As you will notice, Marquez plays with names, their phonetic value, and their repetition. Impossible family lines are drawn and accepted. This is the blurriness of the possible/impossible stated earlier. Typically, in magical real novels, genealogies such as these are offered up ahead of time. This permits the text to ground in the code of the real, the families and their lineage. In fact, Gerald Martin specifies:

> *One Hundred Years of Solitude* . . . can justly lay claim to being, perhaps, the greatest of all Latin American novels, appropriately enough, since the story of the Buendia family is obviously a metaphor for the history of the continent since Independence, that is for the neocolonial period. More than that, though, it is also, I believe, a narrative about the myths of Latin American history. (Martin 1987, 97)

In Barcelo's genealogy—although not drawn out and offered at the start of the text but rather explained over a dense four pages of text—the names and their possible associations are ludicrous, enticing, and fun, as illustrated above.

Where *One Hundred Years* states historical facts marked by temporal anchors (such as the "The American Fruit Company," the workers' strike, and the presence of airplanes and Americans) the novel manages to elaborate a temporal linearity. Barcelo also does this. But then again, he does so not to stabilize the sense of the reader, but to lure him in, as if by trickery. In *The Tribe* it is the primitive Clipocs, some 5,000 years before our era, who invent hockey and Ski-Doos. Sadly, it is out of boredom that they chose to destroy them.

## THE AUTHOR IN THE TEXT

In *One Hundred Years*, it is Melquiades who writes parchments even after his *deaths*, haunting still his family's house. He is an emblematic character of the supernatural (of the magical) in magic realism. He also introduces one of the characteristics of magical realism, which is to overtly and openly include or make reference to the act of writing. The appearance of the writer or the act of writing in magical realism is an autoreflexive tool further destabilizing the premise of the mimetic by calling, or bringing into evidence, the very fictional aspect of storytelling. So, in *The Tribe*, we have an overt attempt to further overthrow the mimetic possible. In *The Tribe*, Ksoar, like Marquez's Melquiades, writes on parchment the story of his people In *One Hundred Years*, like in *The Tribe*, if these parchments were to be lost, so would be the history of its people. In both novels, eponymous characters are responsible for this historical record. However, in *One Hundred Years*, Marquez's character appears seldom, whereas, in Barcelo's *The The Tribe*, entire preposterous and comical chapters are dedicated to the voice of the François character.

## Doubling Identities

Marquez and Barcelo engage in onomastic play. In *One Hundred Years*, this allows for the blurriness of the genealogy, but also allows for remarks on the real. In many cases, magical real texts tend to highlight how it is rather the imitable real that is fecund with the strange and unusual (Walsh Matthews 2011, 397). For that matter, magical real novels tend to illustrate the real in terms of the extraordinary.[6] Conversely, truly extraordinary, miraculous, and impossible events are simply stated, reduced to banal occurrences. To have a series of men named Aureliano on a family tree is in fact not magical or impossible at all. However, when they are 17 brothers, all sons of the same Colonel, all assassinated on the same day (also *possible*), what is strained is the certainty of locating the line between the codes.

Barcelo plays the same game by naming women of the tribe: Mahi (or Mahii, Miha, Mihaa. Mahii Mahii, Marie-Marie, etc.). Furthermore, Barcelo has twin brothers whose names shift constantly (from Pogo and Bogo, to Mogo and Sogo, to Rogo and Dogo, etc.).

## Jokes and Sociocriticism

Playing with history and other elements of the novel allows for the magical realism of Marquez to bring to light important social elements, it's true. However, it is not necessary for the reader to recognize all (if any) of the numerous historical, political, or cultural allusions. In fact, Marquez's novel is a ludic take on the novel . . . this is Marquez's genius, as literary critic Gerald Martin has duly noted.[7] By blending the fascinating with ideology, the incredible with the real, the novel speaks to many. One does not need to feel or understand the greater implications at the socio-critical level to agree that magical realism is entertaining and fun. In fact, such a reading may make it all the more amusing! The same can be said of *The Tribe*. Its literary games and jokes point in all directions, and no one is safe from its derision and dissent. All in good fun, mind you.

Naturally, I am not the first to crown magical real texts with the quality of humor. Much of the work on Borges, Marquez, and Rushdie already adeptly demonstrates how humor is used as a mediating force between the horrors of the past and the uncertainty of the present. Many theorists have devised and entertained readings in terms of the rhetorical maneuvers of the genre or its poetic tools. It is, however, the play with history combined with a sociopolitical discourse that connects magical realism to postcolonialism. What is successful is the potential for play and discovery, the challenge to outdo, to outnumber, to go well beyond Marquez's one hundred years. If criticisms abound and are revealed, the pleasure of the text remains the magical realist novel's greatest asset. And as it has now been almost a hundred years since the boom (and I am joking . . . only a little less than 70), it is time that magical realism takes stock of its influence on literature. As many of its most celebrated authors have won the Nobel Prize and other literary prizes of great note, the effect of mimicry will significantly impact the genre and its continuity. None can deny, however, that magical realism seems to be most prominent where literature, like its people, have felt the need to voice something . . . which I can safely assert is most anywhere that literature can be found, where stories can be found. . . . And where laughter also exists.

## NOTES

1. For a full discussion of theory and analysis of magic realism and further commentary on *The Tribe* see Walsh Matthews, Stéphanie, *Le Réalisme Magique dans la littérature contemporaine québécoise*. For additional reference to the grotesque and magic realism, please see Walsh Matthews, Stéphanie, "On Being Grost-Out."

2. Many theorists of magical realism have noted inherent qualities of the postcolonial in the text. As I have stated, magical realism can be postcolonial, but not necessarily so.

3. This chapter was originally written as an oral presentation in 2009 (before the publication of my doctoral thesis entitled *Le Réalisme magique dans la littérature contemporaine québécoise).* Illustrations and elements of this chapter are further detailed in the thesis (written in French).

4. In my thesis, I propose a chapter on the rationale of the terms "genre" versus "mode," providing an overview of the notion of "genre" as per Todorov's work on the fantastic and the important theoretical ground for magic realism as laid out by Amaryll Chanady.

5. Evelyn Fishburn, "Humor in Magical Realism . . . ," p. 155.

6. As stated in Walsh Matthews, 2011: "The genre has an uncanny way of making the real seem more extraordinary and the supernatural ongoings the most banal structured events one could read."

7. Gerald Martin, "On 'Magical' and Social Realism in Garcia Márquez," p. 97.

## BIBLIOGRAPHY

Angulo, Maria-Elena. 1995. *Magic Realism: Social Context and Discourse.* New York: Garland.
Ballesteros, F. June 14, 2006. "Cien años de soledad," GNU.
Barcelo, François. 1981. *La Tribu.* Montréal: Éditions Libre Expression.
Bowers, Maggie Anne. 2004. *Magic(al) Realism: The New Critical Idiom.* New York: Routledge.
Chanady, Amaryll. 1999. *Entre inclusion et exclusion.* Paris: Honoré Champion.

Chanady, Amaryll. 1985 *Magical Realism and the Fantastic: Resolved Versus Unresolved Antinomy*. New York; London: Garland Publishing.

Danow, David K. 2004 (1995). *The Spirit of Carnival: Magical Realism and the Grotesque*. Lexington, KT: University of Kentucky Press.

Durix, Jean-Pierre. 1998. *Mimesis, Genres and Post-Colonial Discourse: Deconstructing Magic Realism*. London: Palgrave MacMillan.

Faris, Wendy. 2004. *Ordinary Enchantments: Magical Realism and the Remystification of Narrative*. Nashville, TN: Vanderbilt University Press.

Faris, Wendy, and Lois Parkinson Zamora, eds. 1995. *Magic Realism—Theory, History, Community*. Durham, NC: Duke University Press.

Fishburn, Evelyn. 2005. "Humour and Magical Realism in *El reino de este mundo*," *A Companion to Magical Realism*, Stephen M. Hart and Wen-chin Ouyang, eds., pp. 155–167.

García Márquez, Gabriel. 1970. *One Hundred Years of Solitude*, trans. Gregory Rabassa. New York: HarperCollins. [Translation of *Cien años de soledad*, 1967.]

Hancock, Geoff. 1980. *Magic Realism: An Anthology*. Toronto: Anansi Press.

Hancock, Geoff. 1987. *Invisible Fictions: Contemporary Stories from Québec*. Toronto: Anansi Press.

Hart, Stephen. 1982–1983. "Magical Realism in Gabriel Garcia Marquez's *Cien años de Soledad*," *Inti* 16–17, pp. 37–52.

Martin, Gerald. 1987. "On 'Magical' and Social Realism in Garcia Marquez," *Gabriel Garcia Marquez: New Readings*, Bernard McGuirk and Richard Cardwell, eds., pp. 95–116.

Roussos, Katherine. 2007. *Décoloniser l'imaginaire: le réalisme magique chez Maryse Condé, Sylvie Germain et Marie NDiaye*. Paris: L'Harmattan.

Sangari, Kumkum. 1987. "The Politics of the Possible," *Cultural Critique* 7, pp. 157–186.

Scheel, Charles W. 2005. *Réalisme magique et réalisme merveilleux—Des théories aux poétiques*. Paris: L'Harmattan.

Slemon, Stephen. 1995. "Magic Realism as Postcolonial Discourse," *Magical Realism: Theory, History, Community*, Lois Parkinson Zamora and Wendy B. Faris, eds., pp. 407–426.

Todorov, Tzvetan. 1970. *Introduction à la littérature fantastique*. Paris: Collection Poétique.

Vautier, Marie. 1991. "La Révision postcoloniale de l'histoire et l'exemple réaliste magique de François Barcelo," *Études en littérature canadienne* 16.2, pp. 39–53.

Vautier, Marie. 1998. "Magic Realism and Postcolonial Challenges to History: George Bowering's *Burning Water* and François Barcelo's *La Tribu*," *New World Myth: Postmodernism and Postcolonialism in Canadian Fiction*. Montréal; Kingston: McGill-Queen's University Press, pp. 202–253.

Walsh Matthews, Stéphanie. 2012. "On Being Grost-Out." In K. Haworth, J. Hogue, and L. Sbrocchi, eds., *Semiotics 2011: The Semiotics of Worldviews*. Ottawa: Legas, pp. 394–402.

Walsh Matthews, Stéphanie. 2011. *Le Réalisme magique dans la littérature contemporaine Québécoise*. Dissertation, University of Toronto.

*Chapter Six*

# Revising the Myth

*A Proposal for a Methodological Protocol for the Study of American Culture*

## Aida Roldán García

Appealing to the veracity and legitimization that personal experience might play sometimes within the course of argumentations, I allow myself to take the liberty of departing my essay from my personal experience regarding American Studies and the research of a methodology. Because of my previous experience in the study of culture and identity formation, I know that the study of a culture is a complex process in which multiple methods are needed to explore the diverse and, sometimes, contradictory relations between cultural works, practices, the creation of meaning and subjectivity. For similar reasons, I believe that the attempt to define the subject matter of a discipline committed to the study of a specific culture seems too much of a great deed, if we take into account that cultures are not fixed entities, nor is meaning. Agreeing with Joel M. Jones, American Studies' compulsive search for a methodological and subject matter consensus seems to me a utopia, and I wonder up to what point scholars should dedicate their efforts and careers to discuss these subject matters in such terms.

In my view, it is necessary for American Studies to dispose of all positivist reminiscences which still link fixed systematic and objective methodologies to the legitimacy of knowledge. Because meaning is never fixed, Americanists do not need to be "captured, enraptured, and enthralled by . . . *the myth of methodology*" (Jones 1979, 383). Discussions on methodology are bound to continue within American Studies because of the contributions they make to the field, not to pursue a unique, agreed universal methodology to legitimate the discipline and its knowledge production.

To answer Henry Nash Smith's question, "Can American Studies develop a method?" I would like to state that the discipline can indeed develop not only one, but many methods.

Actually, it is methodological plurality what will give scholars access to meanings beyond the range of simplifications and homogenizations of quantitative and objective approaches (Nash 1999, 6). What I suggest in this essay is not a set of pre-established interdisciplinary methodological combinations, but a methodological protocol based on critical and analytical frameworks, which intends to offer scholars a broader field of action to elaborate their own methodologies. The procedure that I propose derives, on the one hand, from my experience in the study of cultural identity construction and representation, meaning, and popular culture genres. On the other hand, it emerges from four main discussions that I have identified while studying the latest trends and turns regarding methodology and American Studies: interdisciplinarity, the transnational turn, the domestic focus and border thinking/consciousness.

My aim is to portray through the critical examination of each of these discussions, which criteria and analytical focuses should scholars use in their study and critique of America and its culture. In order to do that, I will divide the text in different sections, each one centered in one aspect. To make it more visual, I invite the reader to picture my theorization as a diagram in which an Americanist is looking through a magnifying glass how objects of analysis go passing on a conveyor belt through two different analytic frames. The sight of the scholar being conditioned by a border consciousness, the magnifying glass being an interdisciplinary lens, and the analytic frames being a domestic and transnational focus.

## INTERDISCIPLINARITY

In agreement with authors such as Shelley F. Fishkin, Mary Helen Washington and Paul Lauter, I believe one of the most important aims of American Studies is to understand and analyze American culture from a critical perspective, as part of a political and activist compromise and responsibility towards the improvement of America:

> It is up to us, as scholars of American Studies, to provide the nuance, complexity, and historical context to correct reductive visions of America. Whenever people with power act on visions of America that rest on oversimplification, myth, and a blind faith that America is always right or, for that matter, always wrong—that is a call to us as American Studies scholars to do our work. (Fishkin 2005, 20)

Part of the discipline's mission is then the critical examination of power structures and how they work at different levels in the construction and negotiation of meanings and discourses, not only about cultural production and consumption, but also regarding issues of gender, race, class, sexuality and other forms of social difference. The problems arrive when deciding which methods are the best to carry out with these studies.

In 1957, Henry Nash showed the complexities of studying meaning and the limitations of scientific and social sciences quantitative methodologies when applied to humanities and the study of art and culture.

> Social scientists seem to proceed ordinarily as if certain tangible values inherent in society were the only values that need to be taken into account. They find their reality in observed fact, and like all other scholars they have defined facts as the data which their methods of inquiry enable them to discover and record. . . . The procedures of content analysis do not seem to be adapted to the analysis of works of art . . . the content that is analyzed is too rudimentary. (Nash 1999, 6)

Throughout the years, similar claims against simplification and homogenization of quantitative objective methodologies has led Americanists to embrace more qualitative approaches in their researches. First, because due to the lack of fixed systematic procedures, qualitative approaches have given researchers the freedom to determine which methodologies to use when conducting their studies. Second, and linked to this lack of pre-existent procedures, scholars are free to mix and incorporate different and diverse methods and theories belonging to different disciplines. Third, qualitative methodologies have provided more accurate tools and theories to approach and analyze cultural artifacts and practices, since they take into account something essential: the subjectivity of meaning and its relation to historical and social conditions.

> The meaning of a cultural form and its place or position in the cultural field is *not* inscribed inside its form. Nor is its position fixed once and forever. . . . The meaning of a cultural symbol is given in part by the social field into which it is incorporated, the practices with which it articulates and is made to resonate. What matters is *not* the intrinsic or historically fixed objects of culture, but the state of plan in cultural relations. (Hall 1998, 41)

From Hall's words we can yet infer another major reason to reject the exclusive use of quantitative methods: the instability of the discipline's subject matter. As Paul Lauter states, "What is American and what is not?" has as many answers as "what does that mean, American Studies?" (Lauter 2001, 2). The point is then, that American Studies' objects of study are neither fixed nor stable. On the contrary, they are intimately related to the evolution of American cultural identity and what the population, institutions and media identify as American within concrete historical and spatial contexts: "Precisely because identities are constructed within, not outside, discourse, we need to understand them as produced in specific historical and institutional sites within specific discursive formations and enunciative strategies" (Hall 1996, 4).

Nevertheless, to state that American Studies' analysis of culture needs to be interdisciplinary in nature and rely exclusively on qualitative approaches is not totally accurate, since quantitative methodologies have proven to be useful in certain occasions. To illustrate my argumentation, I am going to use feminist cultural studies as a concrete case of how an interdisciplinary approach and a combination of qualitative and quantitative analysis can be really fruitful in the study of American cultural artifacts.

During the first stages of feminist cultural studies, the second-wave feminist sector focused on the study of images and representation of women, directing its attention to mainstream American culture and media. Its objective was double. On the one hand, to criticize the nature of feminine (patriarchal) representations; and on the other hand, to propose and foster positive and alternative images and cultural practices for women (Walters 1995, 24). Those first analyses have been criticized by feminist cultural scholars for different reasons, one of them being the simple and homogenous procedure they followed during their researches: they based their conclusions on statistical methods that only measured feminine presence within the media and culture—books, films, commercials, magazines, etc. The greater the number of feminine characters, the better. By doing that, they disregarded deeply how those representations were portrayed and the complex meaning relations contended in them. Regarding qualitative approaches, cultural feminists have also problematized methodologies based exclusively on this perspective, by arguing that they are too subjected to the criteria and the interpretation of scholars.

The final solution to these problems has been to combine both qualitative and quantitative methods from an interdisciplinary perspective. For instance, scholars analyzing feminine narrative genres are deploying a combination of textual with audience and reception analysis to explore topics such as the construction of the feminine identity and the emergence of new femininities. By learning things such as who consumes these texts and how, they can have a better scope of the complex relations between texts and readers, the different meanings within the narratives and, by extension, their social and political repercussions in identity construction processes.

## THE TRANSNATIONAL

Historical events and processes have always been accompanied by changes in the way we conceive the world. In academia, these shifts have also been accompanied by new theoretical figurations and modes of thought. For instance, the decolonization period gave way to post-colonialist theory. Towards the end of the twentieth century and the beginning of the twenty-first, there was a need for a new epistemological reconceptualization, this time due to the new globalized era and the changes going on under it. As Fishkin suggests, transnational exchanges—whether cultural, economic or social—are not new to these times (2005). However, it is within current globalized contexts that transnational phenomena have turned much more evident to scholars and disciplines:

> It is a moment in which in-depth transformations of the system of economic production are also altering traditional social and symbolic structures. . . . This shift entails the decline of traditional sociosymbolic systems based on state, the family, and masculine authority. As Inderpal Grewal and Caren Kaplan point out, postmodernity corresponds to a reorganization of capital accumulation in a transnational mobile manner. Given this new historical trend toward "trans"-national mobility, it is imperative for critical theorists and cultural critics to rethink their situation and their practices within this scheme. (Braidotti 1994, 2)

As it had happened previously with multiculturalism, post-colonialism and post-nationalism, American Studies has incorporated this new transnational turn into its corpus. Whether as explicit or as a subtext, this turn has changed Americanists' relationship with their work, objects of study, disciplinary protocols and fields in which they conduct their researches (Pease 2011). In other words, researches have been brought beyond national territories, subjects of study have been widely broadened, and new comparative and methodological approaches have been brought to the field.

The collection *Re-Framing the Transnational Turn in American Studies* is an example of one of the many transnational conversations and "views from *el otro lado*" (Fishkin 2005, 23) that have been taking place among Americanists around the globe during the last decade. Despite the reticence this anthology might generate,[1] I would like to highlight and focus on two key ideas developed within it that I find relevant and useful for American Studies: the articulation of the transnational turn as an *interpretative framework* and its prospects at a theoretical and political level. In his essay "Re-Mapping the Transnational Turn," Donald E. Pease focuses on how in the last decade "transnational American Studies scholars dismantled the foundational tenets and premises informing the methodology, periodization, pedagogy, and geographical locations of U.S. American Studies" (Pease 2011, 3).

I understand the title of Pease's essay "re-mapping of the turn" as a clear reference to the evolution and changes suffered by this disciplinary turn in the last ten years. That is, from its origins as a conceptual reorientation of American Studies as Shelley F. Fishkin presented it in 2004, until present-day new formulations as an interpretative and critical paradigm.

From a methodological point of view, the intercultural, mobile and hybrid characteristics of this framework allow the development of methodologies to explore power structures and formations at a transnational scale. At a social and economic level, scholars deploy this approach to elucidate power structures and explore their role in the regulation of global economic and social processes. For instance, how neoliberal capitalist apparatus control wealth distribution; how transnational organizations and institutions organize society; and how discourses on race, gender, ethnicity, class and other social differences are negotiated and formulated. At a cultural level, this approach has given scholars new ways to explore cultural artifacts, practices and processes along with their ideological implications and the agents intervening in their production, consumption and reception. In the essay "American Studies as Mobility Studies: Some Terms and Constellations" we see how a transnational standpoint allows scholars to explore how cultural processes and their meanings might be the result of global operations. Its author, Rüdiger Kunow, proposes a methodology which consists of placing cultural artifacts and practices within networks of relationality with the aim of learning how their meaning is constructed within these net connections and the discursive power behind it.

The search for new ways of approaching culture from a transnational stand view has driven scholars to adopt an interdisciplinary focus. That is, to look into other fields and areas of study to find methods and strategies to address these new analytical challenges. In their study of a new transcultural phenomena in the United States—the emergence of Chick Lit subgenres: Chica, Sistah and Asian-American Lit[2]—Pamela Butler and Jigna Desai combine both feminist cultural theory and racial cultural critique with a transnational perspective. The interdisciplinary focus leads them to connect issues on gender and sexuality with ethnicity and race, whereas transnational feminist critique provides them with tools to address how these issues engage questions related to the nation-state, globalism and capitalism.

Other authors who insist on the importance of interdisciplinarity when studying American culture are Mark Priewe and Paul Lauter. Both of them agree on the benefits of an open dialogue between American Studies and Ethnic Studies, a discipline which according to them can provide Americanists with new concepts, theories and methods to study culture and society from a transnational angle. In their texts "Resistance without Borders" and "American Studies and Ethnic Studies at the Borderlands Crossroads," both authors use the work of the artist and scholar Guillermo Gómez-Peña to highlight the potential of concepts such as the border metaphor, cross-border interaction and cultural hybridity. They maintain that looking into "in-between" and marginal spaces, where the stability of meaning and discourses become suspended and contradictory, can provide scholars with interesting specific information. Something similar we can read in Donald E. Pease's "Introduction: Re-mapping the Transnational Turn."

> In locating sites—borderlands, intersections and junctions—where the inside and the outside of "America" and other cultural domains are intertwined, and where more than one location, tradition, or practice comes into play, transnational discourses have changed the ways in which Americanists imagine their disciplinary objectives and the practical contexts for the articulation of their scholarly projects. (Pease 2011, 6)

They use Gómez-Peña's theorizations because he employs this kind of spatial focus at a theoretical and methodological level in his academic and artistic works. For example, in some of his performances, Guillermo Gómez-Peña creates hybrid spaces with the aim of opening new places of dialogue. He uses spatial anomaly and anonymity to create safe places where the audience can participate and interact freely with cultural symbols, racial and ethnic discourses, bodies, and so forth, displayed within the installation. While the audience is encouraged to explore their relations with Otherness (cultural, racial, ethnic, gender, sexual, etc.), Gómez-Peña is able to gather information about the type of dialogues that arise during the performance, the attitudes of the participants and their interactions and responses to the installation, the different prompts and stimulus.

From my point of view, the versatility of the transnational does not only lie on its methodological formulations, but on the wide range of possibilities that it has at a theoretical and discursive level. For instance, the disciplinary turn has also helped in the formulation and fostering of post-national discourses since it challenges meanings of national belonging and cultural identification: "in transnational formations, identities, things, finances, and places are not bound by national identifications and investments. The transnational does what the border does with the nation: it confronts the nation with its own internal differences" (Pease 2011, 5). This is really useful, for example, in the elaboration of new epistemologies regarding contemporary subjectivity and identity articulation processes.[3]

I believe as well that Americanists, and scholars in general, should use transnational critical theory to articulate post-national discourses to combat new nationalist outbreaks, emerging out of the population's discontent with transnational institutions and nation-state attempts to recover their power and sovereignty. The transnational should be used to formulate new governmental models away from state-power and market-power centralization. That is, models that "undermine the juridical and economic constraints of the transnational state of exception, . . . accomplish the redistribution of economic entitlements and cultural recognitions, and . . . remap geographies (Pease 2011, 38).

## THE DOMESTIC

In "Introduction: Re-Mapping the Transnational Turn," Donald. E. Pease expounds the necessity for American Studies to keep studying as well, social, political and cultural processes at a domestic level. Arguing that these kinds of processes are not exclusively the result of transnational and global forces, he explains how dangerous it is for scholars, under the influence of the transnational turn, to believe that "dominant and subordinate economic and cultural positioning within domestic cultures [are] the inevitable effect of global processes" (Elliott, 2007; Sharpe 2000a; in Pease 2011, 14): ". . . transnational Americanists who encouraged the reformulations of multicultural conflicts that took place *within* nations in terms of the cross-cultural processes carried out *in between* national and transnational imaginaries often ignored the structures of economic and cultural injustice that persisted within the domestic sphere" (Pease 2011, 15). In this section, I intend to develop Pease's idea on the necessity for American Studies to focus on the domestic sphere and the recovery and development of critical frameworks to conduct analysis at this level. Specifically, I will focus on multiculturalism and Ethnic Studies as sources for critical interpretative frameworks to address issues related to power, diversity, and meaning production within American national boundaries.

During her presidential speech to the American Studies Association in 1997, Mary Helen Washington suggested how both American Studies and ASA needed to incorporate Ethnic Studies into their lines. Believing in the political commitment and responsibility of American Studies, she tried to promote an institutional change at a larger scale. Her aim was to end up with social injustice and racial and ethnic discriminatory policies within institutions by fostering transcultural and transracial dialogues and the institutionalization of inter-ethnic, inter-racial and multi-cultural paradigms (Washington 1998, 22). Nonetheless, she hasn't been the only one to suggest this turn to Ethnic Studies to Americanists. As seen in the previous section, we find other scholars who in the last decade have also seen in Ethnic Studies an excellent source of methodological and theoretical tools to study new cultural dynamics and realities within the United States. In my view, though, it is George J. Sánchez, one of the authors, who best attempts to articulate a convincing discourse about the necessity for this interdisciplinary turn.

In his essay "Creating the Multicultural Nation," George J. Sánchez offers a critical analysis of the relationship between Ethnic and American Studies while suggesting a new turn in U.S. multiculturalism. From a post-nation-alist stand, he examines how discussions inside left-wing U.S. academia on cultural and racial diversity are not only pointing dangerously to new nation-alist outbreaks, but also to post-ethnic models of society. After a harsh cri-tique of these models based on institutional equality and "cohesion amidst diversity" (Sánchez 2000, 46), he calls attention to the necessity to keep focusing on the social and economic problems that still threaten U.S. minor-ities and these neoliberal models try to silence. Because these conflicts have a colonial/race/ethnic nature, Sánchez propounds a re-turning and reformula-tion of multiculturalism as a critical framework to address them.

Feelings towards multiculturalism have always been disparate. Whereas some sectors consider it a positive move for minorities in terms of represen-tation and rights, some others consider it a discursive capitalist maneuver to commodify cultural difference. My view is that multiculturalism as a concept has a lot of potential if scholars manage to re-formulate it into a critical paradigm that supports a political spirit of struggle against social injustice. Of course, this reconceptualization should avoid "complicity with logics of neoliberal capitalism" (Pease 2011, 12) and models based on cosmopolitan-ism. A new multicultural framework, forged within Ethnic Studies, would have the power to evidence how hegemonic structures still regulate relation-ships and meanings between ethnic and racial minorities in relation to main-stream national discourses.

Since multiculturalism has "expanded the meaning of cultural differences beyond racism and ethnicity to include gender, class, sexuality, and disabil-ity" (Pease 2011, 14), it is also relevant, then, to combine multiculturalist insights with other critical approaches to examine how cultural and racial differences interact with issues such as gender and sexuality. For example, the application of a multicultural domestic focus and feminist cultural theory to the study of Chica Lit has allowed me to examine how the alternative counter-hegemonic femininities appearing within this subgenre narratives are the result of the clash and dialogue of mainstream Anglo culture and differ-ent national discourses—Chicano, Puerto Rican, Cuban, etc.—on gender, ethnicity, femininity, the body, sexuality, and race.

But the (re)turn to the domestic, Ethnic Studies and multiculturalism is not only justified by the critique of power structures and the construction of racial and ethnic meanings at a domestic level. Sánchez's discussion contin-ues with the criticism of a new form of nationalism based on neoliberal values and cosmopolitan and post-ethnic discourses, promoted by U.S. left-wing academia. This national project, born out of the disenchantment of the left, blames and accuses debates on social diversity, injustice and civil rights movements of the last decades of being a burden that has restrained the American nation and institutions from evolving, and has pushed the popula-tion to the political right-wing (Sánchez 2000). Thus, supporters of this na-

tionalist project suggest to bury discussions on these social issues and encourage academia and institutions to focus on more important things such as
economic change and national unity against adversity.

The problems emerging from this national project are several. On the one
hand, the fact that the state would have full control of the regulation of
construction and representation of social differences would mean that discourses would be under the domain of a regulating apparatus that, at the same
time, is controlled and pressured by the demands of larger transnational
power structures such as the market. In practical terms, that would mean that
social difference and multicultural agendas run the risk to be elaborated
under the interests of these hegemonic power structures. On the other hand,
the cosmopolitan and ethnic models lying under neoliberal nationalist, far
from looking for social equality, just try to hide asymmetrical power exchanges happening among the population because of these differences.

In short, U.S. scholars have to make use of both re-formulations of multiculturalism and the re-turn to Ethnic Studies to elaborate domestic multicultural agendas based on social injustice critique and equality within the U.S.
To base these agendas on cosmopolitan and post-ethnic discourses would
mean that academia is falling into a fallacy which puts at the same level
institutional equality and actual social reality. In my view, the use of neoliberal nationalist cultural imagery and ideological claims—"cohesion amidst
diversity"—is not a naïve, utopian attempt to improve society. Very much on
the contrary, scholars supporting these ideas end up naturalizing, installing
and maintaining differences among the population, and being accomplices of
capitalism and other transnational institutions processes which try to obscure
economic, social and political inequalities (Lauter 2001, 133).

## BORDER THINKING

The last component of my methodological protocol for American Studies is
"border consciousness." This concept coming from Gloria Anzaldúa's text
*Borderlands: The New Mestiza* refers to a new political proposal which engages a new kind of subjectivity and a new way of inhabiting the world based
on border-crossing. Thanks to the re-formulations made by different authors
and its use by different disciplines and studies, the concept has evolved and
developed into what today is known as border thinking. To end my proposal,
I will explore briefly the role that border consciousness and thinking has had
at a general level inside academia and within American Studies, and why it is
so important for Americanists.

In 1987 Gloria Anzaldía wrote: "Because I, a *mestiza*, continually walk
out of one culture and into another, because I am in all cultures at the same
time, *alma entre dos mundos, tres, cuatro, me zumba la cabeza con lo*

*contradictorio. Estoy norteada por todas las voces que me hablan simultáneamente"* (Anzaldúa 1987, 99). In that text, she celebrated the birth of a new kind of subject born out of ambivalence and cultural clashes— Mexican, indigenous and American—whose hybrid and flexible conditions allowed her to adapt to the different contexts and realities in which she moved. The term "border" was also re-signified in this text: it went from referring a mere national limit to becoming an exclusive space where all kinds of dialogues, struggles and negotiations could take place. The conceptualization of this new way of inhabiting and conceiving the world has given light to a set of new theoretical figurations in relation to the subject, the body, space, relationships, and so forth, which have provided academia and disciplines with new meanings and knowledge.

In the last decades we find different theorists who use concepts similar to Anzaldua's mestiza and border thinking. Scholars such as Rosi Braidotti have used the adjective "nomadic" to talk figuratively about individuals who embrace a mobile consciousness and "relinquished all idea, desire, or nostalgia for fixity" (Braidotti 1994, 22). Despite that Braidotti's nomadic consciousness does not correspond exactly to Anzaldúa's proposal, it relates undoubtedly to it in the sense that it stands up on the same values—hybridity, transition and mobility between categories: "The nomadic subject is a myth, that is to say a political fiction, that allows me to think through and move across established categories and levels of experience: blurring boundaries without burning bridges" (Braidotti 1994, 4). The "yearning consciousness" theory proposed by bell hooks is more similar to Anzaldúa's model in the sense that it works "as an affective and political sensibility which cuts across the boundaries of race, class, gender, and sexual practice and that could be fertile ground for the construction of empathy—ties that would promote recognition" (hooks 27; in Braidotti 1994, 2).

In American Studies there have been several authors appealing to border thinking in the last decade. For instance, Mary Helen Washington stated in "Disturbing the Peace . . ." that "liberation requires border crossing" (Washington 1998, 13). In his text "American Studies and Ethnic Studies at the Borderlands Crossroads," Paul Lauter focuses his discussion on the "borderland" metaphor from a theoretical and methodological point of view. He illustrates how border metaphor, thinking and theory have given light to theorizations and conceptualizations of culture and national identities much more plural and multiple, according to new cultural and spatial realities (Lauter 2001). The border thinking Lauter encourages American Studies to embrace embodies a new consciousness that require scholars to learn how to inhabit a political and ideological position of constant border-crossing. Besides decentralizing and reconfiguring American Studies' agendas and focus of attention, this new way of inhabiting and moving through categories, discourses and levels of experience is supposed to lead scholars to new meanings and re-significations resulting from new dialogues, discussions and negotiations.

In the same way that Lauter sees in border thinking new ways of performing cultural and political activism, I believe Americanists have to internalize a border consciousness as part of the political project and agenda of American Studies. Because social and cultural equality cannot be gained through laws made by the States and based on post-ethnic theories, American Studies, academia and institutions need a new mentality that really fosters a democratic culture; that is, a culture that doesn't consider immigrants as aliens but pleads for cross-cultural dialogue and alliances, even if that entails to keep dealing with issues of history, culture, post-colonial heritage, white supremacy and national identity. In my view, it is the task of Americanists to support a process of awareness within society which recognizes the new socio-cultural realities within the country and the need for new ways to approach "the Other" and open spaces of transcultural dialogue. However, in order to participate and take a stand in this process towards a new mentality, scholars and academia have to first embrace and interiorize a border consciousness.

In conclusion, at this point of the discussion I recognize the necessity for American Studies to continue with debates on methodology. I find it extremely relevant to keep proposing and conceiving new ways of addressing America from different flanks, not only because of the mobile nature of meaning, but because of the exceptional conditions emerging from the new world order. Because proposing a single methodology would not be enough, my attempt within this essay has been to propose a methodological protocol. What I have suggested has been a set of critical and analytical frameworks and focus that I find essential in the elaboration of any methodology. The interdisciplinary is a lens that allows the scholar to carry out studies from different perspectives. The transnational and the domestic focus provides a better knowledge on how power relations work in the construction and negotiation of meaning and at the same time provides theoretical paradigms for the construction of post-national discourses. Finally, border thinking and consciousness promotes and encourages scholars "to learn to think differently, to invent new frameworks, new images, and new modes of thought" (Braidotti 1994, 1).

## NOTES

1. Contrary to what its editors claim, the discussions within this anthology only offer a limited examination of the historical significance and academic prospects of the transnational turn within American Studies. One of the reasons for this limitation is that despite that all the discussions deal with different issues, they all share the same academic, temporal and spatial background. Hence, these debates are representative to that specific background, and not to a

larger scale as the anthology claims it does. Another reason is the notorious lack of works dealing with race, ethnicity and gender issues within the collection.

2. Chica, Sistah and Asian American Lit are Chick (girl) Lit (literature) subgenres addressed to specific ethnic and racial feminine audiences. Chica (girl in Spanish) Lit for Latinas; Sistah Lit for African American women; and Asian American Lit for Asian women.

3. Rosi Braidotti and Zygmunt Bauman are two examples of authors who have theorized about postmodern subjectivity and its mobile, unstable and multiple character. They have both suggested different models to illustrate it: in *Nomadic Subjects: Embodiment and Sexual Difference in Contemporary Feminist Theory* (1994) Braidotti chooses the figure of the nomad whereas Bauman prefers the figures of the pilgrim, the tourist and the vagabond in his text "From Pilgrim to Tourist—or a Short History of Identity" (1996).

# BIBLIOGRAPHY

Anzaldúa, Gloria. 1987. *Borderlands: The New Mestiza = La Frontera*. San Francisco: Spinsters/Aunt Lute.

Braidotti, Rosi. 1994. *Nomadic Subjects: Embodiment and Sexual Difference in Contemporary Feminist Theory*. New York: Columbia University Press.

Butler, Pamela, and Jigna Desai. 2008. "Manolos, Marriage, and Mantras: Chick-Lit Criticism and Transnational Feminism." *Meridians: Feminism, Race, Transnationalism* 8.2: 1–31.

Fishkin, Shelley F. 2005. "Crossroads of Cultures: The Transnational Turn in American Studies: Presidential Address to the American Studies Association, November 12, 2004." *American Quarterly* 57.1: 17–57.

Fluck, Winfried, Donald E. Pease, and John C. Rowe. 2011. *Re-framing the Transnational Turn in American Studies*. Hanover, NH: Dartmouth College Press.

Hall, Stuart. 1994. "Cultural Identity and Diaspora." *Colonial Discourse and Post-Colonial Theory: A Reader*, edited by Patrick Williams and Laura Chrisman, 392–401. London: Harvester Wheatsheaf.

———. 1996. "New Ethnicities." *Stuart Hall: Critical Dialogues in Cultural Studies*, edited by David Morley and Kuan-Hsing Chen, 441–449. New York: Routledge.

———. 1998. "Old and New Identities, Old and New Ethnicities." *Culture, Globalization and the World-System: Contemporary Conditions for the Representation of Identity*, edited by Anthony D. King, 41–68. Minneapolis: University of Minnesota Press.

———. 1996. "Who Needs Identity?" *Questions of Cultural Identity*, edited by Stuart Hall and Paul Du Gay, 1–17. London: Sage.

hooks, bell. 1990. *Yearning: Race, Gender, and Cultural Politics*. Boston, MA: South End Press.

Jones, Joel M. 1979. "American Studies: The Myth of Methodology." *American Quarterly* 31.3: 382–387.

Kunow, Rüdiger. 2011. "American Studies as Mobility Studies: Some Terms and Constellations." *Re-framing the Transnational Turn in American Studies*, edited by Winfried Fluck, Donald E. Pease, and John C. Rowe, 245–264. Hanover, NH: Dartmouth College Press.

Lauter, Paul. 2001. *From Walden Pond to Jurassic Park: Activism, Culture, & American Studies*. Durham, NC: Duke University Press.

Nash Smith, Henry. 1999. "Can 'American Studies' Develop a Method?" *Locating American Studies: The Evolution of a Discipline*, edited by Lucy Maddox, 1–16. Baltimore, MD: Johns Hopkins University Press.

Pease, Donald E. 2011. "Introduction: Re-mapping the Transnational Turn." *Re-framing the Transnational Turn in American Studies*, edited by Winfried Fluck, Donald E. Pease, and John C. Rowe, 1–48. Hanover, NH: Dartmouth College Press.

Priewe, Marc. 2011. "Resistance without Borders: Shifting Cultural Politics in Chicana/o Narratives." *Re-framing the Transnational Turn in American Studies*, edited by Winfried Fluck, Donald E. Pease, and John C. Rowe, 265–279. Hanover, NH: Dartmouth College Press.

Sánchez, George J. 2000. "Creating the Multicultural Nation." *Post-nationalist American Studies*, edited by John C. Rowe, 40–62. Berkeley, CA: University of California Press.

Walters, Suzanna D. 1995. *Material Girls: Making Sense of Feminist Cultural Theory*. Berkeley: University of California Press.

Washington, Mary H. 1998. "'Disturbing the Peace: What Happens to American Studies If You Put African American Studies at the Center?': Presidential Address to the American Studies Association, October 29, 1997." *American Quarterly*. 50.1: 1–23.

*Chapter Seven*

# Envisioning Global Citizenship

## Ifeanyi A. Menkiti

In considering the situations described by the usages: "post-colonial," "diaspora," and "globalization," and the subsequent question "where do we go from here?" it seems to me exceedingly important that we first make clear whether the diaspora is seen as preceding the globalization, or the globalization the diaspora. If we begin, as we should, with the idea of the "post-colonial," a recommended trajectory, and one most serviceable, would be to go forward from the stage of globalization, and not forward from the stage of diaspora. Of course, it all depends on how one sees the journey, and where one thinks it best for humankind to be going at this point in time. In the way that I have conceived of it, and would like to propose in this chapter, globalization should be seen as preparing us for the final stage of globalism, by which I mean the globalism of ethical citizenship. Given that colonialism and its aftermath are usually seen as a bad thing, judging from the ethical point of view, the badness of what happened is bound to have some mitigation, if, at the end of the journey, the world's different peoples were finally able to come together in an ethical commonwealth, having learned a few lessons along the way.

An observer of our contemporary scene, which, no doubt, is still noticeably full of conflicts, might however understand things differently, stating that such an ethical commonwealth is not possible; that the human tribes of the world, being hostile to each other, are irredeemably fractious and unyielding; and cannot be courted on to submit themselves to a global will where ethical governance is the issue.

But is ethical governance on a global scale truly impossible, or is it our own failure of the imagination that makes it appear impossible? The failure of progress on this front may have more to do with our various imaginative failures than it does with what is actually the case on the ground. So, let me suggest a different trajectory to the journey, keeping in mind my main position which is the view that globalization without an attendant globalism creates a situation which is ethically indefensible.

First came Colonialism and then came the Postcolony, and with the postcolony the spreading around of peoples called the Diaspora. Globalization is situated within a network of certain antecedents. Now, for us today, there is talk of the globalization of industry; and of globalization regarding the marketing of goods and services beyond the borders of an originating country.

The main point for all of us, right now, is that in a very real sense everyone is currently occupying each other's space. The inheritors of village society are rubbing shoulders with the inheritors of industrial society, and there is no end in sight to the rubbing. Very often cognitive conflicts arise.

Consider the following example. In several of the big cities of the West, whether it be New York City, London, or Paris, the people I have called the "inheritors of village society" (many of them immigrants or longtime transplants from the old world) are engaged in a mutual life with the native sons of the industrial West. Both sides are currently playing the game of a new industrial culture.

But negotiating the *content* of what's right and what's wrong is not always easy between the two sides. The Westerners, for instance, demand "transparency" and "impartiality" in the administration of justice; and often think of the new arrivals from the old world of Asia and Africa as tending to be biased and nepotistic when they engage in public hiring. The Westerners do not realize that the issue may be more complicated in regard to the ethics of the situation. These descendants of the old world are not necessarily being biased or nepotistic when they lean towards "hiring their own." They may well be thinking of the demands of the new order as a strange sort of arrangement.

In the old village, the people you work with are people you know, people who are known to everyone else. Hiring from a blind list, and promoting from a distance (as the new industrial culture demands), is a strange way of proceeding because men and women intent on safeguarding the public good, as in the old village, just don't do that. You need to know the quality, as well as the character, of the person to whom you are entrusting things. No one who takes the village assets seriously would ever consider going in an impersonal direction. "Transparency" "impartiality"—how does one translate these terms so that they have meaning within the context of an old culture whose descendants are now settled within the bounds of a new country?

It seems to me that the newly arrived who have been accused of partiality and other things are perhaps more disoriented than they are biased or nepotistic. They do not necessarily mean to be despoiling the public treasury of a new place for the benefit of their kinsmen from the older place. The problem may have to do with this: Which idiom, which usage, are we deploying to get a handle on the justice issue?

This issue of the relevant frame of reference may seem like a dry academic question, but it has deadly consequences in real life. Consider the recent example of the claimed use of chemical agents in Syria by the regime in power. One can well imagine the Syrian president, Bashir Assad, saying to himself in response to the charge that he had used such weapons on his own people that he did no such thing. He could say: "What are these Americans and Europeans talking about? Maybe, my generals put gas on the people, but the people they put the gas on are *not my own people*. If they were my people, they would not have historically brutalized the Alawites who are my people; the Americans and Europeans do not really understand the ins and outs of peoples in this part of the world; they have not even understood it in regard to themselves."

Under this scenario, it is self-defense of the ultimate kind; and any reference to liberal international values falls short of solving the problem. Here, again, it still appears to be that old question: Whose justice, whose rationality, are we talking about? And who has the right of final speech regarding the declaration of judgement as to whose justice, whose rationality should prevail?

Now consider this other example of a white taxi driver and a black passenger who is trying to flag him down in an attempt to get to a black neighborhood. The black passenger is a well-paid professional; is able and willing to pay; usually he tips generously. But the white taxi driver is afraid to stop. He is afraid he might be mugged, erroneously mistaking the black professional as a potential thug, a common thief scheming to pounce on a hapless white cab driver.

Here, in this example, there is fear in place in one place and insult in place in the other place. Is the white cab driver reasonable in his fear regarding his safety; and is the black passenger not reasonable in his own feeling that he is being subjected to an insulting discriminatory practice? An impartial objective observer, looking at the question, is not an inch closer to coming up with a single algorithm, a single reasonably adjusted scheme of moral accounting by which the interests of the white cab driver and the interests of the black passenger could be balanced out, one over the other. Is the white cab driver to be blamed for being afraid? Is the black passenger not entitled to feel insulted at what he sees as an act of discrimination? Whose discomfort should outweigh that of the other; and how do we conduct the measurement?

In considering the earlier problem brought up regarding the Syrian president, I do not think it is very helpful to fall back on a reference to the detailed rules of the international order, insisting that rules are rules and that rules are the only guarantors we have of justice across the globe. For here, coincidentally, we are reminded of that joke about the accountant who was fond of saying: "I only deal with rules and regulations and with documents; I do not deal with reality."

The point one is trying to make is that there are, or should be, some more substantive considerations beneath the formulated rules. Which means that the parties should, as far as possible, come at issues from the same or similar vantage points. Otherwise, we could wind up having exchanges such as this:

> Speaker 1: You wicked soldiers of the enemy force. We shoot with rubber bullets to scare you, but you shoot with real ones. How unchristian of you to do so.
>
> Speaker 2: We do not have anything against you. But war is war and church attendance is a different thing. We will embrace each other after the war is over, but not before.

It is said that during the Second World War, with the movement of the German divisions into the eastern front, towards the Russian heartland there was the felt sense of atavistic antagonism; an insinuation that it was no longer Europe fighting against itself but rather two different peoples fighting against each other—the Teutonic tribes against the Slavic; hence it was okay to unleash wholesale terror by one population upon the other. Eastern Europe was not really Eastern Europe but the name of some other place, the Germans were said to be proposing.

But we do know that Eastern Europe is not east of Europe; it is centrally part of Europe. Of the region, we say that it is not an outlier to a place called Europe; and we also say, in the same breath, that Central Europe, though considered the center of Europe as drawn on a map, still does not mean that the rest of Europe is subordinated to it in regard to the substance of history.

Geography is what it is, but history and group affiliation often get to trump geography depending on the situation one is facing. As a result, locational designations notwithstanding, when it came to the intensity of the vehemence between Germany and Russia during the War there may have been more to the story than originally met the eye. This is not of course to suggest that an unbroken unity existed among the Slavs, nor suggest that an unbroken unity existed among the Teuts. But there was enough such unity for us to justifiably think of advancing a classification along those lines.

Since wars are generally mean and nasty we all need to do our best to understand their causes and what pushes them to go one way rather than another once hostilities break out. There is very often a tendency to think that the problem of war and conflict is a civilizational one; that as humanity moves away from its tribal past, and rational achievements accumulate, war would become a thing of the past.

In this regard, thinking here of the distinction between First World and Third World, the assumption, obviously a civilizational one, has always been that the sooner Third World peoples give up their sense of tribal affiliation and the raw emotions that come with such affiliations, the better for them and their affairs; and the better for the affairs of the rest of the world. Third World, in other words, should become like First World. Learn some rationality and the discipline that comes with the restraints of law.

But, here, one runs counter to the historical evidence. For what the US national elections in 2016 shows us, with its elevation of an unexpected president, is that the distinction between First World and Third World is not set in stone. First World can become Third World overnight; can even become Fourth World were there such a classification. The raw emotions of an angry public; the shameless defacement of the symbols of authority; the bizarre spectacles occuring on a daily basis—these things were indeed unexpected, happening as they did within the bounds of a territory designated First World. Historians will most likely be spending many years trying to untangle what happened to the presumed rationality of a political order two hundred and more years in the making.

There is today, among the liberal peoples of Europe and America, a deepening feeling of sadness, perhaps a feeling of despair, regarding what appears to be the world's unending divisions and ill will—the feeling, judging from the US elections, that real change is not ever going to happen. But in my mind, we have to assume that it is not true that real change is not ever going to happen and that conditions will never be in place for good things to come. We globalists must remain optimists. Our world need not be condemned to an unquenchable tribalism, either of the European or Third World variety.

Consider, for another example, a situation of a large extended white family inside the United States of America, the plurality of whom have traveled extensively around the world and have many friends from all over the globe—black, brown, yellow, and other shades; Africans, Asians, and folks from the South Pacific come and go in visits to this extended family's household.

But there is one dissenter in this household who is not comfortable with being around members of other races. The dissenter says to himself: What is wrong with the rest of my family that they cuddle up to people not of their own kind? Or the dissenter might look inside and, after looking inside, maybe one day say to himself: I must have been conceived by Martians who gave me a load of bad genes, genes so quarrelsome and dismissive everything is now a problem between me and the rest of my family.

My point here is that a moment of truth soon inevitably dawns on each and every one of us, at some time in our separated lives, and then we have to figure things out for ourselves. And part of this figuring is to confront the nature of our relationship with others.

In the foregoing example, it may be noted that the recalcitrant member of the extended household in the story was never ever guilty of violating any laws regarding the rights of those he had considered strangers in the land. He fully complied with all the laws prohibiting violence against them; and fully played the clinical game of what I once elsewhere called "justice as arithmetic."

However, when we found ourselves moving from the zone of "justice as arithmetic" to the zone of justice as real justice, human respect became a key part of the picture. And with respect as part of the picture, the things we were looking for came to be more substantive, reflecting, as they do, a deeper engagement with the claims of the human person.

The considerations which arise in our quest for justice as real justice might sometimes appear to be problematically open-ended, but that is no reason for the philosopher not to pursue things in this direction; seeking to establish what may count as the parameters of genuine justice in the world.

Call this "justice of the heart," as distinct from a justice of the mind; or justice as arithmetic. The main point is that we also have to think of the affective part of the practices that sustain human equality; the emotional contours of the territory occupied by our various talks concerning just equality.

There is, in this regard, an interesting argument which could be made— that in denying black people equality in the United States, white people, in effect, are not thereby able to make equality work among themselves. This claim is made on the grounds that for an idea to be apprehensible, it must have behind it a sustaining practice. An idea is empty without the sustaining practice which is needed in order for it to be comprehensible (i.e., understood). A damaged practice is not able to sustain its originating idea, but is instead sidetracked into sustaining something else—something quite different from what was originally planned.

Here, in other words, it needs to be said that there is a cost to the idea of justice, and the cost is a certain level of adequacy in the practices we deploy when pursuing justice. For example, if the idea of gunpowder precludes the practice of leaving the powder and the flintlock out in the open air with the spring rains coming down, philosophers should not be surprised if the claim is made, as it is here being made, that justice and equality are also conditioned by the practices that give them heft. Justice and equality would not be what they are said to be absent a certain quality in the underlying practices that we have put in place to sustain and secure them. Practical violations have practical consequences and practical consequences have consequence for the purity of the original idea.

I should additionally mention that this notion of the connection between the adequacy of a sustaining practice and the pureness of the original idea may also be found relevant in the international arena where talk exists of the need for justice to flourish among nations. We know that the expression "the family of nations" is not the same thing as the expression "the families of the nations." With the latter, divisions could continue to insert themselves into the management of things, as we move to a higher international order where certain patterns of the earlier loyalties could themselves become a problem by standing in the way.

The various nations, understood as families, become a problem when we propose the idea of "the family of nations." A unity implied at one level becomes problematic in the light of another kind of unity being sought. We could say that if the nations want unity *between* themselves they may have to tailor down the idea of the unity *within* themselves.

It is perhaps for this reason, that some authors in the field of Rawls scholarship have been tempted to go straight into a global original position, bypassing the notion of peoples altogether, whenever matters of international justice arise.[1] I am alluding here to John Rawls' philosophical notions of the two Original Positions. But, as I am tempted to argue, this is a wrong move; peoples still matter, though not for the reasons that they are said to matter, traditionally speaking. In order to reemphasize, I want to quote the definition of the Second Original Position of John Rawls: "At the next level, the idea of the original position is used again, but this time to extend a liberal conception to the Law of Peoples. As in the first instance, it is a model of representation, since it models what we would regard—you and I, here and now—as fair conditions under which the parties, this time the rational representatives of liberal peoples, are to specify the Law of Peoples, guided by appropriate reasons" (John Rawls 1999, 32).

But Rawls aside, my point here is that within the international arena, there are now certain usages and expectations regarding what may or may not be done between peoples; that these usages and expectations are forming the basis of a practice; and the emerging practice is gradually structuring the idea of international justice.

Quite often, the prospect of international peace appears daunting to the observer. And if the observer is a religiously minded philosopher, he might go on to put his faith in the God of creation, who will not fail us; his thinking being that regardless of the conflicts we face, our God, simply, will not abandon us to a fate of mutual destruction. To which one might add that everyone is indeed allowed to guess at God's plans so long as the guess is reasonable guess, for reasonableness itself is a gift from the God who made us.

The theologian who proposes this approach is certainly in a good position to gain allies in the field of philosophy. The theologian's God is not an alien entity to the practitioners of philosophy. There are commonalities between the two fields—as witness the extensive philosophical literature bearing on the ontological arguments and the metaphysics of existence; the question of beingness in reality not just in thought—the *de re*, not just the *de dicto*, of the quarreling schoolmen. We are allowed to guess at God's plans, and when we do, what we might find could be additional evidence towards the conclusion that humanity is moving in the direction of an ethical equipoise. Our job then is to make sure that we do not prevent such an equipoise from coming into being through our own preventable failures of the imagination.

The Hebrew prophets talked of the "Tikkun Olam"—that is, the need for there to arise those who repair the world. "Tikkun Olam" in Hebrew, or in English "repairers of the world," calls attention to the need of human agency in advancing the goals of creation. It is not that God can't do it alone, if he wanted to; but that the situation is more fulfilling if we can do it together with God.

Thus we should encourage the young child to grow into responsible adulthood by showing the child appreciation so that he or she can grow in confidence. We should treat the young child as entitled to appreciation and the things that redound to an appreciated child, such as the feeling of respect and self-acceptance. We are saying to the young child: be the best you can, for God wants you to be the best that you can be.

If the message sinks in, the child grows in self-acceptance and self-confidence and the taunts of the bullies in the schoolyard will not bring him down. This is part of the "Tikkun Olam" mandate, if I have understood it correctly.

But then, even here, to attempt to repair the world or heal creation, as mandated, means that we must have hope. If the world was a place of irreversible damage, what is the point of even trying? We must have hope and look at the positive, enabling, side of things, to the extent possible.

When some people point at history, for example at the incalculable sufferings of the victims of Stalin's Gulag, they tend to repeat the mantra: "What is the point of even trying to heal or repair the world; humanity is broken, fundamentally broken."

But is it not possible to say of Stalin that, left alone to himself, he never wanted the Gulag; that with various antecedents in place he was forced to embrace the Gulag? The idea here is that since certain things happened, and other things happened in response, the Gulag became an option and was subsequently enforced by the Stalinist machinery of state. Stalin, the historian might here argue, was not necessarily unreasonable and unfair in the matter of what he did since he could have been trying to protect himself from certain slaughter; trying to do what he felt he had to do to keep from collapse the Soviet state. And here the unintended consequences of prior societal action becomes one way of explaining, though not necessarily, of justifying things.

It was important to bring up the Stalin example because his was not a case of hostile populations fighting against each other, but rather of cruelties spun off within a single population. My idea is to fight the view that if "brothers" can do this to one another, then what is the hope that one can erase the divisions between groups, between races or cultural groups? I do not necessarily mean my observations to count as a way of explaining away the Stalin question, except to say, once more, that men and women must remain hopeful wherever, and whenever, they find themselves confronting these issues.

And sometimes humanity has had to use the gift of humor to get a handle on the discomforts arising from our various conflicts. It is as if with humor we might be saying to ourselves: well, then, if we can't solve our problem by the dint of our intelligence or the dint of our compassion, then let's try something else.

The comedian who tickles his audience by asking the question: "when yoga people die, can they go to the Christian heaven?" is no doubt coming at it from a point of view which he finds laughable and would like others to so find, namely, the view that Christians are over here, and Hindus over there; and there exists an existential gap between the both of them. And we can also here well imagine this same comedian asking himself and others the question: What if the heavenly candidate before us is a person, who was once a Baptist, but is now a yoga practitioner answering to the Hindu faith? The question then, in changing nuance, becomes: Can a former Baptist turned yogi still be able to go to his Christian heaven? With this, we immediately enter the possibility of permutations not on a single tree, but permutations advancing on different trees. There would be no end in sight to the visibility provoked by the comedian's initial question. Here, in other words, we sometimes have to laugh at our foibles to keep ourselves from going crazy, caught, as we often are, in the middle of our various unnecessary wars.

Some say that globalization has intensified the problem of race; others that globalization positions us to render race a thing of the past. Whatever one's position on the matter, let me make a quick point regarding the racist and his dilemma.

It has occurred to me that the racist is able to make race matter only from the outside. He has to step out of his own skin to commit his racial acts. But then, when he does, he is no longer the white-skinned person he deems himself to be. What he sees, from the outside, is a racial amalgam, a white mass of individuals whose bodies are, in terms of color, by itself, quite indistinguishable one from the other.

And the number of these amalgamated bodies, the resurrected and the currently standing; the long gone under earth's lid and the alive who survived them; plus the future to come—billions of white bodies (or billions of black bodies, for that matter)—witnessing all of them, the individual man or woman who started off by feeling racially privileged is bound to ask: What is so special about this super-abundance of white bodies? This surfeit of nature, what is so special about the reiterated presence of these physical bodies, whether they be designated as white.

Absent the requirements of culture, the requirements of value and spirit formation; of the companionable reaching out by entities who are not just bodies but persons, what this color-fixated racialist witnesses happens to be an overwhelming mass of physical bodies who are not responsive to a code. Meaning remains absent from his mix of things.

And until we add to the mix an interior world in which, as "spirit seeking light and beauty" we avow that there is more to us than bones and skin-color, nothing should matter to him or to us. We are called upon to give reasons, at least for some things if not for others.

Persons are not meaning-making and they refuse to be reduced to a mere accounting by way of color-rated physical bodies. The racialist is only able to do the racial thing by standing outside his own skin; and, when he does, what he encounters is a spooky thing, an unsettling spectacle. As with white racists, so likewise with the black racists.

Again, in order for the racist to realize the grandeur of the beauty of his own preferred white or black skin, he has to be able to stand outside himself. He has to be able to stand outside his own skin, playing the observer looking from the outside in, not a subject looking from the inside out. This presents a conundrum, and is a mental maneuver not easy to accomplish; it is perhaps one of the reasons why serious racists appear to be also seriously mentally compromised. The health of the mind and health in one's moral relations with others appear to be somehow linked.

I suppose that one other way to re-state what I have been aiming at, all along in this essay, is to call attention to what I have elsewhere called "the powers of the symbolic universe." It must surely have occurred to many of us that our world is full of symbols; and that these symbols, though created by humans, have force beyond anything imaginable by those who created them.

The grip of the symbolic universe, its determinative force, needs to be addressed. The Secret Service agent throwing his body on that of the president, his willing readiness to take the bullet on behalf of the president because the honor of his people, gathered in a historical space, was what was at stake. The agent does not do this for reasons of money alone; the last thing on his mind could not have been that his salary will be increased if he successfully protects the president.

The US Marines who are symbolized as the toughest of the tough, as hanging in there till the bitter end; the Sibling Division of the Indonesian Forces; the Gurhka Rifles who know what honor demands; and so on, and so forth—these are all part and parcel of the symbolic universe; and the symbolic universe has its grip. A detached age of impersonal relations talks in clinical fashion of contracts and signatures, of quid pro quos, not of honor or of the symbolisms of a situation. "Hard calculations," the age insists; but then ignores the underlying motivations that produce the hard results. Oaths are taken, and ceremonies surround these oaths; and both oath and ceremony are not inert.

Something internal in the human being, an urge answering to the pull of symbolic forms, appears to be producing palpable results in the social world where rational calculations of the sort usually advanced do not produce such a result.

But regardless of the yield of palpable results, it needs to be acknowledged that in our new globalism what is at stake is primarily the building of new attitudes—new attitudes of respect towards the human person. Our goals should primarily be focused in the area of attitude change. Even though results are also important, we want the results to come from the right kind of underlying attitude. It is not being suggested that our choice is one of attitude-based vs results-based; but rather one of engendering the right kind of relationship between the two. Our main concern, and one which is fundamental, is the equality of human persons, and with it the building of a world in which everyone feels that they count; and that they, too, carry weight. In the end, it is not just a matter of abstract philosophy, but of lived lives. For people generally know when they are being treated with respect; they do not need a dictionary to tell them when they are being dis-respected. Respect is the key job of the new globalism.

Therefore, turning now to something set in a more positive place, and with an aim to bringing this paper to a close, let me point out that the defenders of globalism in our age should also be aware of the power of the arts to push forward the agenda of globalism. They must be prepared to call upon the various arts and the creative life, generally, in their very attempt to usher in a new era of collective harmony in which the world's peoples live together in peace.

Folks doing music together, do not have time to kill each other. Their brains are not in a destroying mode; nor is agitation part of their brains' operational chemistry. Specific ins and outs exist for all our various activities. Philosophers and artists should take note.

Rabindranath Tagore[2] is one writer who was fully aware of the importance of music and the arts in the civic and political lives of peoples. And the world is better for his wisdom—the world not just of Asia, but the world of the rest of us. In closing, therefore, let me end by quoting the last segment of my long poem "Mutatis Mutandis" which is the opening poem of the collection, *Of Altair, the Bright Light*:

> the earth is where we live;
> the earth—it is
> the one place we may call home.

# NOTES

1. I am alluding here to John Rawls' philosophical notions of the two Original Positions. First, Rawls suggests explaining his theory of the First Original Position: "Before beginning the extension of the liberal idea of the social contract to the Law of Peoples, let us note that the original position with a veil of ignorance is a model of representation for liberated societies. In what I am now calling the first use of the original position, it models what we regard—you and I, here and now—as fair and reasonable conditions for the parties, reasonable and rational citizens, to specify fair terms of cooperation for regulating the basic structure of this society" (30).

2. In *The Religion of Man*, delivered as Hibbert Lectures in Oxford, Tagore writes, "Our life gains what is called 'value' in those of its aspects which represent eternal humanity in knowledge, in sympathy, in deeds, in character and creative works. And from the beginning of our history we are seeking, often at the cost of merely for the success of life. But when this creative ideal which is *dharma* gives place to some overmastering passion in a large body of men, civilization bursts out in an explosive flame, like a start that has lighted its own funeral pyre with boisterous brilliancy" (Tagore 1922, 145–146).

# BIBLIOGRAPHY

Menkiti, Ifyeani. 2005. *Of Altair, the Bright Light*. Chelsea, MA: Earthwinds Edition.
Rawls, John. 1999. *Laws of the Peoples: With "The Idea of Public Reason Revisited."* Cambridge, MA; London: Harvard University Press.
Tagore, Rabindranath. *The Religion of Man*. 1922. London: George Allen and Unwin Ltd.

# Index

123

# About the Contributors

**Paget Henry** is professor of sociology and Africana studies at Brown University, with a special interest in the Caribbean. He is the author of several books including *Peripheral Capitalism and Underdevelopment in Antigua* and *Caliban's Reason: Introducing Afro-Caribbean Philosophy*. He is also the editor of *The CLR James Journal* and *The Antigua and Barbuda Review of Books*.

**Markus Arnold** is associate professor of French and Francophone studies at the University of Cape Town. He holds a bi-national German-French doctorate on Comparative/Francophone literature, has taught at ENS Lyon, ESA Reunion and University Reunion where he is research associate (LCF EA 4549). His interests cover Francophone and comparative "Global-South" literatures and cultures (notably Indian Ocean), postcolonial theory, graphic literature (*bande dessinée*) and contemporary cinema. His publications comprise the monograph *La littérature mauricienne contemporaine: Un espace de création postcolonial entre revendications identitaires et ouvertures interculturelles* (2017) and the co-directed book *L'image et son dehors: contours, transitions, transformations* (2017). He currently works on the publication of the co-edited volume *Indian Ocean: Ecotones, Contact Zones and Third-Spaces* (2020), "Afropolitanism," and the relationship between *bande dessinée* and contemporary art.

**Melanie Otto** is assistant professor in postcolonial literatures in the School of English at Trinity College Dublin. She has published on Caribbean writing, the work of Keri Hulme, and visual art, contributing chapters to *Rhys Matters: New Critical Perspectives* (2013), *Landscapes of Liminality: Between Space and Place* (2016), and *Caribbean Literature in Transition, Vol.*

*1* (forthcoming 2020). Publications in journals include essays on plantation landscape in the work of Kamau Brathwaite and Annalee Davis (*Journal of West Indian Literature*, April 2017) and on poet-shamanic aesthetics in the writings of Wilson Harris and Gloria Anzaldúa (*CLR James Journal*, December 2017). Together with Lee M. Jenkins at University College Cork she has co-edited a special issue of *Caribbean Quarterly* on Irish-Caribbean Connections, published in the autumn of 2018.

**Stéphanie Walsh Matthews**, PhD, is an associate professor in the Department of Languages, Literatures, and Cultures in the Faculty of Arts at Ryerson University in Toronto, Canada. She is currently the Director of the Arts and Contemporary Studies Program as well. Currently, her research areas include language, evolution, artificial intelligence, autism spectrum disorder, and semiotic theory. She continues to be interested in social semiotics and literary criticism and considers genres such as magical realism as a key indicator of the intrinsic conveyor of a societal voice.

**Aida Roldán-García** is a researcher and a language teacher. In 2011 she obtained a BA in English philology and in 2013 she got an MA in construction and representation of cultural identities from Universitat de Barcelona. Currently she is a PhD candidate at University of Massachusetts–Amherst and works as a Spanish teacher in Barcelona. Her areas of interest are U.S. Latino/a literature and culture, gender studies, and cultural studies.

Born in Onitsha, Nigeria, **Ifeayni Menkiti** first came to the United States to attend Pomona College for his undergraduate degree. Later he went on to Columbia University and New York University for further studies. He received his PhD in philosophy from Harvard University. He has taught philosophy at Wellesley College for more than 30 years and is currently a professor emeritus there. He is author of three collections of poetry, *Affirmations* (1971), *The Jubilation of Falling Bodies* (1978), and *Of Altair, the Bright Light* (2005). In 1975, he was honored with a fellowship in poetry from the Massachusetts Council on the Arts and Humanities through the Artists Foundation, followed in 1978 by an award from the National Endowment for the Arts. Menkiti's poetry has also been aired on National Public Radio, WBAI (NYC), and WGBH (Boston).

# About the Editor

**Ashmita Khasnabish** earned her PhD from Bowling Green State University, Ohio, and MA (group A) in English literature and MA in (group B) literature and linguistics from Calcutta University, India. She was a Research Scholar in The Asiatic Society, Calcutta, India, before coming to the United States for her higher studies. Currently a lecturer at Lasell University, Boston, she held many research positions as a visiting scholar at the Massachusetts Institute of Technology, Brandeis University, and Brown University for the last two decades, and taught at Lesley University, Emerson College, and Boston University. Dr. Khasnabish authored three monographs entitled *Jouissance as Ananda: Indian Philosophy, Feminist Theory and Literature* (2006, 2003), *Humanitarian Identity and the Political Sublime: Intervention of a Postcolonial Feminist* (2009), and *Negotiating Capability and Diaspora: A Philosophical Politics* (2016, 2013). She published many articles in refereed journals and contributed many book chapters in edited volumes, and lectured widely in Europe, North America, and India. Recently she held the position of visiting scholar in Oxford University's English faculty and delivered her lecture on her book project on virtual diaspora. She is also a fellow of the Royal Asiatic Society, London. She will be in Oxford University in October (2019) as a visiting scholar, and her article "The Theory of Liberated Love and a Global Feminist Discourse" will be published in *Angelaki: Journal of the Theoretical Humanities* 25, 1–2 Special Issue; Love and Vulnerability: Thinking with Pamela Sue Anderson (January 2020) and also as a hardback book by Routledge in 2020.

www.ingramcontent.com/pod-product-compliance
Lightning Source LLC
Chambersburg PA
CBHW022325280326
41932CB00010B/1228